Blanche Willis Howard

Dionysius

The Weaver's Hearts Dearest

Blanche Willis Howard

Dionysius
The Weaver's Hearts Dearest

ISBN/EAN: 9783744673341

Printed in Europe, USA, Canada, Australia, Japan

Cover: Foto ©Thomas Meinert / pixelio.de

More available books at **www.hansebooks.com**

Dionysius the Weaver's Heart's Dearest

BY

BLANCHE WILLIS HOWARD

AUTHOR OF "SEVEN ON THE HIGHWAY," "THE OPEN
DOOR," "GUENN," "ONE SUMMER," ETC.

NEW YORK
CHARLES SCRIBNER'S SONS
1899

Dionysius the Weaver's Heart's Dearest

I

BETWEEN the Danube and the Neckar, high in the bleak hill country known as The Rough Alp, perched the hamlet Hexenfels. Grim rocks grouped in evil counsel dominated the barren land; peasants' flat roofs would have whirled away were they not freighted with heavy stones; and nothing — man, mouse, or moss — could well exist unless hardy enough to defy the long sweep of icy winds that battled here with fury all unspent, though they had rushed from the far frozen north across a continent.

Close behind the poor cottage of Dionysius the weaver towered the Witch-Tooth, a formidable crag, sparsely overgrown with patches of straggling bushes, vines, stout small leaves, and a few flowers of undismayed temperament. The child Vroni — born naughty —

when sent in the legitimate course of things
to feed hens was wont to dash off to the allur-
ing rocks and loiter royally.   Climbing swift
and sure where seemed no foothold for a goat,
she busily would amass a large store of treasures: leaves, bits of moss, an owl's feather, a
trailing stem quite bare but good for skipping-
rope, a gaunt wiry stalk most excellent for a
switch, and from the crevices pretty arabis.
Always seeking to grasp more, she would let
fall and lose her precious hoard, since desirable things were legion, and of greedy little
hands she had but two, — these indeed in great
demand, — as, monkey-like, she clung, hung,
swung, and lifted herself along her zig-zag
course.

In midsummer she would venture high, and
higher, for gay wild pinks, — "weather-pinks,"
say the Suabian Highlanders, — until recalled
to earth by her irate mother down below,
shouting, when fate willed, against the wind,
and clapping soundless but portentous palms.
The great chiding voice was now so wee and
impotent, the powerful stature so unintimidat-
ing, the child felt bound to stop short, hold
her sides and laugh, flinging down from her
eyry peals of wicked glee and mockery, —

floating haply on the wind, — while ostensibly scrambling earthward, yet never too fast for manifold dalliance with brambly delights. Vroni herself was not unlike a mountain pink, — bold, lithe, lawless, vivid in color, careless of wind and weather.

Perchance a stray goat, chased from afar by some breathless peasant lad, and overtaken at last in these witchy wilds, first traced with inconsequent nibbling the site of Hexenfels. Surely no less erratic, no more responsible spirit ever could have chosen so inhospitable a spot of earth for the struggle for life, and even a moderately well-endowed goat ought to have done better for himself. Had the place possessed conceivable advantages, the ruins at least of a feudal castle would have haughtily affirmed them. But not even a *Pots-Blitz* robber knight had found it worth while to establish in this desolate region the lofty and lineal seat of his depredations.

Far from the high-road, difficult of access, unmolested by tourists, quite beyond the strenuous hum of modern progress, Hexenfels remained what it had been for centuries, an isolated and humble community of toilers. Thirty mean cottages, or rather huts, with

their clumsy, stone-laden roofs; dulness, tame-
ness, dreariness beyond words, pessimistic
fowls slowly strutting across a dirty street, an
oppressive torpor, a singular dearth of popu-
lation: in short, a squalid travesty of the
sleeping palace of enchanted beauty, and nothing at all alive except the mind, — thus would
the urban stranger who never arrived behold
Hexenfels.

Yet here dwelt by no means wretchedly a
sturdy folk, cherishing with gallant obstinacy
its bleak home, solemnly tenacious of its prejudices, its own social code, its gradations of
worldly dignity, and drawing a certain stubborn strength and pride from the deep-rooted
traditions of an historic past.

No tyranny as to top hats obtained in Hexenfels, no rigid conventions as to the color
and cut of a man's coat at certain appointed
hours of the day, no stern law as to the width
of his trousers and the angle at which he
should shake hands, no Draconic code decree-
ing gloves or no gloves. But, in other details,
perhaps equally essential to the well-being of
humanity and the growth of the soul, Hexenfels was not a whit less arbitrary than London.
The points of view differed, that is all.

Had you sought to persuade Vroni Lindl that her environment was squalid, her existence joyless, she would have laughed in your face. In the earlier and peculiarly unregenerate stage of her being, she might indeed have startled you with a response even less civilized than her impish laughter, and it would have been a hopeless task to convince her that cooped-up town children, the miserable limitations of whose sad dull days afforded no Witch-Tooth as background of the universe, were to be viewed with aught but contemptuous pity.

It must be admitted of things really worth having she had her share. The few crooked, hump-backed, sour plum-trees by the back door, — what child worthy of the name would fail to perceive at a glance the inexhaustible versatility of those stunted and delightful objects? Round the feeble vegetable garden before the front windows stretched a bristling unkempt hedge of lilac, elder, and wild white hawthorn, beneath which in the spring time she found rare and most wonderful violets. In the great pile of wood and fagots, always, winter and summer, just beyond the hedge, she scooped dim and fragrant hiding

places and crouched breathless, in an ecstasy
of mystery, when none pursued. She dili-
gently wove willow-twigs into her thickly
wadded winter petticoat to make a most surprising crinoline. The clayey soil which
sorely tried the patience of her elders minis-
tered only to her joy, for she never wearied
of moulding flowers and figures, and drying
them in the sun. Her father smiled at her
creations; but her mother sniffed and called
them idle trash.

Finding snails in the woods after a rain —
either for home consumption or to sell at the
rate of a hundred for twenty-five pfennigs —
also added zest to her existence. Whether
swinging in the delectable barn, or rioting on
the haymows in the meadow, or construct-
ing fine couches of moss in the forest, no
child was ever keener in pleasure, none ever
plunged with more tingling life and ardor
into the business of the moment.

But, alas, not all the little girl's pursuits
were reputable. Once with splendid though
misdirected zeal, in sheer wrath and revenge,
— a pure vendetta spirit indeed, — she, aided
by another like unto her, — it was the " red
Lisl," — walled up with stones and wood and

earth two tiny casements suggestively near
the ground, so that a weeping and exasperated
old crone was obliged to light candles in
broad daylight when she came home from
church. For this enormity — in spite of its
undeniable genius, and a certain classic simplicity in thus effectually shuffling a growling and meddling beldam out of sight as
if she were a recreant vestal virgin — little
Vroni received from her good father six dozen
on the hands with a big pewter spoon.

Perhaps her most memorable exploit was
to set fire to a heap of hemp and pith under
her neighbor's, the "*Distel-Bauer's,*" great
walnut-tree, which, the season being dry, began
to blaze terrifically and amazingly, and had to
be extinguished with buckets and hose like a
veritable house a-fire. The village children
naturally gloried in the flash of inspiration
that had created a prank of such dimensions;
but the men and women spoke their minds
without wincing, — as was the fashion in
Hexenfels. When one dwells on wind-swept
heights exposed to the ravages of a Vroni
Lindl, silence ceases to be a virtue, and a
sound shaking of the culprit, if by good luck
you can catch her, seems no more than one's

duty to the commonwealth.   The year of the
flaming walnut-tree was perhaps the most agitated epoch of Vroni's early chronology.

She saw her father, Dionysius the weaver,
— so called in contradistinction to Dionysius
the cobbler, — a pale dark man in gray drilling clothes, a leather apron, and a soft black
cap with a visor, working at his loom in the
front room early and late.   Great piles of
bed linen and table linen the father wove,
drilling too, and sometimes linen for aprons.
Only in an emergency of harvest, haying, or
sowing, did he join the others in the field.
The farming as well as the work of the small
household was done by his wife, aided finally
by Vroni only, as the older brothers and
sisters went gradually, one by one, out into
the great world, far away from the humble
nest in the shadow of the Witch-Tooth.

Dionysius, a simple man, peasant born, had
rather gentle ways and a soft mode of speech.
Some of his neighbors said he was never
aught else.   Others declared he had learned
things in Vienna, where, when he was young
and lively as a colt, he had gone to live with
a bachelor uncle, and ply the weaver trade.
It was hinted the uncle had thought the world

of Dionysius, and meant to leave the boy all his money, but lost it and died suddenly, nobody ever quite knew of what, or how, or where, or when, — and Dionysius returned to Hexenfels, changed and "quiet-like," with nothing to say for himself. There he remained, working steadily at his trade, married twice, and harmed neither man nor beast.

Yet some pretended, so lamblike as he seemed, he had been a rare wild fellow in Vienna, and he and the young uncle naught but a godless pair of rogues, weaving more mischief than honest warp and woof. These, however, were at worst dim and fluttering rumors such as may follow saint or sinner, and never really current in the village; while the prestige of that all-but-inherited fortune clung to Dionysius, imparted to him a certain romantic distinction, and formed a stable topic of conversation in a community where, as in most rural districts, people conversed comfortably only upon oft-digested themes. As he, laboring to feed the many mouths under his roof, grew ever paler and began to stoop more than his age warranted, they were wont to say: —

If Dionysius the weaver's uncle had not,

etc., then Dionysius the weaver would now, etc., etc., and in spite of the logic of facts, the struggling family at the Witch-Tooth seemed always in public estimation the more opulent for those fugitive and largely mythical avuncular possessions. But in the weaver's brooding memories the loss of money played no part.

Vroni adored her father. He had a way of looking at her with his soft brown eyes that was potent beyond the roughest blustering and sternest threats from other quarters, or even than actual chastisement. Worse still was his way of not looking at her. That was the one punishment she could not endure. That quite broke her heart.

All the year round, her mother Agathe, bustling indoors and out, wore a loose drab jacket, a calico skirt, and a dark-red three-cornered kerchief tied round her head. She was rough of temper and tongue, of a discontented, fault-finding disposition, but transparently honest, thrifty, cleanly, self-respecting, exacting much of others but more of herself, an indefatigable worker, never accomplishing enough to satisfy her own demands.

While human intercourse seemed to evoke

from her chronic exasperation, she displayed for domestic animals peculiar affection and gentleness, to which they one and all responded. Any music, even the cheapest, transformed her personality, moved her to sudden and extreme gayety, and caused her to throw all care to the winds. But when Dionysius the weaver heard music, his face grew wistful and he remembered his childhood.

Even when but a coltish little lass, Vroni knew instinctively that he was made of finer stuff than the rest of them. But only in after years, and when too late, did she behold him clearly as he was: a man loving justice, firm as the crag when he saw fit, yet of most peaceable intent; mild, tolerant, and pitiful, freehanded, an humble and unconscious worshipper of beauty, and in affection fathomless.

Agathe's greatest pleasure was a good supper not at her own expense. His was a quiet walk through harvest fields, — alone, or hand in hand with his little daughter. Outwardly she resembled him, inheriting his slight frame and small bones, his good straight profile, and his eyes. But he was pale from indoor life,

and she all sunny glow, and what was hidden
in the depths of the child, none could discover
for the bewildering overgrowth of pranks on
the surface.

Agathe conscientiously endeavored to train
her daughter's turbulence into sobriety, and,
was no colossal misdeed convulsing the community, punished her, chiefly by reduction of
rations, for venial and chronic sins: when she
could remember not a word of the sermon,
whispered or giggled in church, and loitered
coming home from school; when she tore her
frock, stole sugar from the pantry or dried
apples from the garret; when she gave pert
answers or shirked her daily tasks. These
even when she was small comprised such
trifles as bringing in armfuls of wood, chopping fagots short for kindlings, fetching three
big pails of water from the brook, driving the
cattle to water, feeding the hens, weeding
the salad, and scouring pots and pans. At
intervals she would dash out of her orbit from
pure erratic mischief, but a worker she was,
skilful, thorough, and swift. Even Agathe
admitted that in this respect the little one
was "the best of the lot," — referring thus
graphically to two older daughters of her

own, and still another, Dionysius's child by
his first wife.

Vroni looked askance at this half sister and
two half brothers, not altogether because they
were grown-ups, but chiefly on account of
their holiness as opposed to her own flagrant
naughtiness. She took them for saints, very
disapproving saints it was true, less gentle
than the pictures in her book, but unmiti-
gated saints nevertheless.

Them too, and her own sisters, she saw
vividly only in the long perspective of years.
Little enough did she consciously concern her
small self with their unimportant personalities. Yet even then her spirit in autocratic
child-fashion was imperturbably gathering and
sifting its own evidence, never the evidence
intended for and intruded upon it by grown
people.

Five great brothers and sisters were still
packed close in the house when she was already
old enough to run about and turn things
topsy-turvy.

First came Sebastian, grimly religious,
almost more austere than any monk. Always
brimful of holy zeal, he longed to quicken
cold hearts with fire and sword. Rash, hot-

tempered, yet warm-hearted and good when
not blinded by religious prejudice, honest to
the core, but that was a family trait.   Falsehood was almost the only naughtiness un-
achieved, nay, unattempted by Vroni.

Sebastian's tiny sleeping place in the garret — room it could hardly be termed — was
monopolized by a staring altar decked with
linen of the weaver's best weaving, a glossy
blue porcelain Virgin trailing a tinsel mantle,
two unlit tallow candles, some gaudy saints
and Sacred Hearts on gilt-edged cards, gar-
lands of arsenic-green wax ivy leaves, and
tissue paper roses many-hued.   Yet honor
and praise to the Rough Alp man.   His sort
is rare.   His shrine, it may be, was not beautiful.   But where was room for only bed or
altar, he sacrificed his ease to his ideal, and
lay upon the floor.

The pious sister Anna was cold and unsym-
pathetic.   In time she drifted to the Swiss
convent, St. Scholastika, where she became
Sister Corona, knew and desired to know
nothing of this vile world, spoke in a toneless voice, and had, even as a woman of fifty,
the manner of any unintelligent child.   Vroni
better liked the irascible Sebastian.

Melchior also was very religious indeed. With eyes raised meekly toward heaven, he yet kept a pretty sharp lookout on this sinful world, was mindful of his neighbor's opinion and careful of appearances, — a harmless fellow, so far as a person who tacks with every breeze can in the long run be harmless. Vroni grew to be fond of him with a half contemptuous fondness. But that was in later years when he was a king's coachman, most discreet, sleek, and respectable, and she far less, from the social point of view.

Of her own two sisters, one was boisterous and quick-tempered like the mother, went away young into service and never came back; while Marie, a gentle girl, married the lame village tailor and soon had her arms full of ailing babies.

Long after all these great ones, little Vroni had come into the world like a gay surprise, as if the embodiment of some merry melody which had floated across the stubbly fields of her mother's laborious existence; or like a fugitive flash of those old Vienna days of which Dionysius the weaver never spoke.

Although Vroni seemed to set at naught her patient, toiling, God-fearing folk, their

influence encompassed her; their stubborn
peasant pride, their integrity was also her
inheritance. They came of good old stock.
All were clean-lived and dutiful — her father,
her mother, her great grown brothers and
sisters. Her grandfather indeed had been
Schultheiss of Hexenfels, which office — making due allowance for differences of proportion — is equivalent in dignity to that of Lord
Mayor of London. Her Tante Ursula still
enjoyed on this account a certain worldly
prestige.

Tante Ursula's was one of the few houses
which could claim the high honor of offer-
ing His Reverence breakfast after mass.
Hexenfels, although proud of its little round
chapel set on a hill, was no regular parish,
but merely a humble station, remote, isolated,
sometimes indeed all but inaccessible. The
care of its souls was assigned to two or three
priests in alternation who came long dis-
tances, often through fierce mountain gales
and blinding snowdrifts, for all great feasts,
for funerals, and usually on every other
Sunday.

Mass was barely over when Tante Ursula
would hurry home to prepare breakfast; good

coffee, white bread and black, fresh honey, and wild rose marmalade. The floors, the tables and chairs had been scoured white with sand the day previous. The one upholstered chair, never profaned by family use, was drawn from its repose to sustain His Reverence. The one china cup and the one silver spoon, incredibly old but ever radiating a sort of virgin splendor, were in readiness.

It was the privilege of Vroni and her rag-doll with bead-eyes to sit on a three-legged stool and stare unblinking at His Reverence drinking from the good cup and stirring with the good spoon. As the same priests for the most part appeared year after year, they grew very fond of their little nutbrown companion. Each, after breakfasting, would take her on his knee, smile indulgently at her un-shy jabber, and give the pretty rogue coffee and all the sugar she wanted. Emboldened by so unassailable entrenchment, Vroni obstreperously churned hard bread-crusts with the precious spoon, — venerable heirloom, thin of constitution and delicate as to the throat — cared not a *pfifferling* for the tragic glances Tante Ursula was shooting at her across His Reverence's tonsure, rudely thumped the deli-

cate cup, piratically demanded and obtained
the forbidden marmalade, and grinned amicably with a naughty smeared mouth at her poor
aunt.

After which episode, Vroni was invariably
asked whom she best loved, and unblushingly
responded *God*, having learned this, like her
courtesy to her superiors, mechanically in her
tenderest years.   It is possible that a strict
but unecclesiastical moralist observing her
goings-on from Monday morning till Saturday
night, and on the Lord's own day no less,
might have taken umbrage at this barefaced
assertion.   Yet after all, it was perhaps
essentially true.   Who knows?   Happily at
any age, we are something better than the
foolish, heedless, mad things we do, and
Vroni through all evil that befell her dearly
loved the light.

As far back as she could remember she
had been no unimportant part of the pleasing
ceremony of His Reverence's breakfast at
Tante Ursula's, where through the years
the selfsame observances followed one upon
another in regular sequence.   It was therefore not surprising that one day she, a glowing, gleaming creature of twelve or thirteen,

and growing very fast at that time, came confidently to her clerical friend, — it was the youngest priest and the one she loved best, — sat herself upon his knee, flung her arm round his neck, and began her free and innocent chatter.

But Father Aloysius very gently put her down, and, patting her hand kindly, said she was rather large now for the old baby ways, would soon indeed be as tall as Tante Ursula. He continued in this wise, affectionately, smiling always, but to the child's dismay calling her Ve-ro-ni-ka.

Vroni, her eyes fixed unwavering upon his face, stood and scowled in silence, deprived of her rights, angry with herself for being big, uncomprehending and incredulous; until suddenly a strangely vague discomfort seized her, she flushed violently and fled, unheeding the priest's friendly call and Tante Ursula's horrified remonstrance.

In this way and at this moment wild Vroni was ashamed for the first time in her life, yet knew not why, or what the ugly sensation was. Instinctively following the great primeval example, she ran and hid herself, — but far more impetuously it is probable than

the example could run.   In the woods, things
grew no clearer, nor yet on the tip-top of the
Witch-Tooth.   A nascent sense of the fateful
instability of pleasant things, a dread of the
loss and peril of change, had been roused in
her by the young priest's gentle rebuff.   Why,
since she liked him and he was good to her,
might she not still sit on his knee?   Why
had he called her Veronika?   Helpless, un-
comfortable, angry, and defiant, she wandered
home.   That night she made herself very
small and young as a young child, and
crouched on the floor, her cheek pressed close
against her father's leg, who silently smoothed
her hair.   But her mother said it was silly
actions, like a dog — which it was.

II

THE narrow table against the wall was small for five persons, but they sat close, elbow to elbow, and the supper took little room. At one end was Dionysius the weaver, next him his wife. The light from an open wick, drawn through a cork floating on beechnut oil in a nicked cup, fell on his pale face and brilliant eyes under his visor, and upon the florid robustness of the woman's contours and her wide cheeks framed by her red kerchief. Vroni, at the other end, devouring potatoes with open-mouthed zest and grinning maliciously at her brothers, was yet vaguely contrasting types and dimly speculating, not with mere fondness, but with rudimentary æsthetic satisfaction, upon the fine sadness of her father's face.

"'T is a nasty wet night and the storm is rising," grumbled Agathe, aggressively loud-voiced, grating her chair on the stone floor and crossing the kitchen with ponderous tread. "*Du lieber Gott!* As if we'd not wind enough! To be sure I've long known an evil blow was coming. My beasties told me. Lightfoot for one has been flying after her tail like mad. When an old cat goes foolish wild and kittenish and plays with herself all alone, mind, not set on by other cats, and narrows her eyes down to two little lines of fire, and leaps high after one knows not what, then look out for a witch-wind."

Taking a lantern from its nail, she began to dig out the remains of a tallow stump.

"Vroni, fetch me a bit of candle. Hast left the lantern filthy again. Art scatter-brained. Art good for naught."

To the dissertation on feline prescience nobody responded, it being familiar as the importunate wail of the blast. Nor did Vroni, inured to more strenuous vitupera-tion, mind in the least the comparatively mild reproof, but, chewing a potato skin with obtrusive nonchalance, fetched the desired candle and asked pertly: —

"Say, mother, didst ever see a live witch?"

"Not I, thank the Lord! A witch brings rare bad luck. A smaller bit, careless child. Wouldst beggar me with thy wasteful ways?

Not that bad luck fails year in year out. Never a witch could bring worse."

"Ah, wife, wife!" remonstrated Dionysius looking up with a faint smile from the shuttle he was mending. His friendly glance resting briefly on his two tall sons, who having come in late were still stooping assiduously over their soup-plates piled high with boiled potatoes, followed the quick movements of his Mädel and lingered lovingly on her bright, dark, impertinent face as she leaned knitting against the wall.

"Art foolish, Mann?" returned Agathe, grimly. "When have we two had aught but ill luck?"

"We've got a roof over our heads at least," he suggested amicably.

With a bellicose snort, she retorted: —

"But would have none I take it this evil night, had I myself not set Sebastian and Melchior a-lugging up fresh stones."

"We have six good children," he suggested with pacific intent; "sober-minded and hardworking," looking at his sons, — "straight-grown and rosy," — smiling well pleased upon his daughter.

"Naught to boast of!"

"We have never lost one, Agathe."

"Is it sense to tell me that?"

"Or seen one wander in evil ways," he added, not without a strain of solemnity.

"Ha! If they went wrong, they'd find they had their mother to reckon with! I'd like to see them dare — the pack!"

"Yet 't is easy," said Dionysius, low, and bent over his shuttle.

"Thou, mother," persisted Vroni, inquisitive yet incredulous, "didst ever really meet an honest body who knew one that, telling no lies, had truly chanced to spy a live witch?"

"Scores, saucebox, and all honest folk. My blessed granny, Heaven rest her soul, saw them eighty years, and that thou knowst well. For often enough have I told how she looked up the very day she died and beheld them racing and shrieking and whirling upside down and playing leapfrog round the Tooth."

"Clouds," meekly interpolated Dionysius.

"Clouds indeed!" cried Agathe, incensed. "Do clouds yell and hoot and curse?"

"Not to my knowledge."

"And tap on the casement and laugh till the blood runs cold!"

"But, wife —"

"If there be no witches, then why is the crag Witch-Tooth by name? Answer me that!" she demanded in triumph. Whereupon the weaver bowed his patient head and attempted no reply.

"If there be witches," declared Vroni, succinctly, "I mean to see one. If there be none, I mean to know it."

"It is not well to be always talking of evil," Sebastian now urged, pushing back his plate, wiping his mouth on his sleeve, and crossing himself deliberately.

Melchior, tolerably skeptical on the witch question, yet inclined in any event to be on the safe side, crossed himself likewise.

"Father," harped Vroni, leaning on his shoulder, "say, are there live ones?"

"Believe or not, there's worse than witches abroad," announced Agathe, with an air of bringing on her heaviest artillery, while removing the empty dishes with a clatter. "Why was the *Distel-Bauer's* hound, he that is mostly mouse-still, baying enough to wake the dead? Why does my brindle low? Why are the young pigs, both Engländer and Ungarn, nosing about at this time of night? Why is the

hencoop in a flutter? Didst mark the flight
of the hawk at sun-down? Hast watched the
signs the ravens show to such as have eyes to
see?" Tramping about, she was yet from
alternate corners always directing her volley
at the inoffensive bowed head.

"Dost not answer? Hast seen naught?
Nay!" she exclaimed with massive scorn.
"Not thou! Willst naught of signs, though
dumb things rise up and speak when the soul
of a suicide—" she crossed herself, Sebastian
and Melchior did likewise—"is flying up from
the lowlands. It is on this wind and no other
that such souls go howling by. 'T is the black
witch-wind and the suicide wind. The soul is
on the way, and until he is past the Tooth no
honest beast can rest. Hark!" Her powerful
figure motionless, she stood with upraised
warning hand.

The rain fell in torrents upon the roof, casements rattled, from all quarters gusts like ham-
mer-blows struck the cottage, while inexplicable
sounds, inarticulate human tones of grief, rage,
and despair, rose, fell, rose again, and surged
upward toward the Tooth.

Dionysius smiled reassuringly upon the spell-
bound group.

" 'T is a rarely exposed site, and the last of October," he ventured to say with a deprecating look at his wife towering still in the shadow.

Vroni, knitting fast, her cheeks flushed, hung breathless over the weaver.

" Is it true, father? Say! Why did he kill himself? How did he do it? Must have been but a poor foolish fellow, eh, father?"

" Seest, wife? Canst fill the Mädel's head with sorry notions," he protested gravely.

" Is a big girl and no swaddled baby more, as thou wouldst have her still."

" Say, father! But a foolish fellow, eh? A silly pate." Vroni nudged him with an imperious elbow.

" A sinner," amended Sebastian's deep chest tone of conviction.

Dionysius flung a restraining arm round his impetuous little daughter, and rejoined slowly : —

" As to that, we are all sinners, and it must be a rarely unhappy one that goes off thus : hard pressed somehow, knows not which way to turn, loses his head quite — poor lad — poor lad ! "

" Speakst soft as though thou sawest him near ! Wouldst defend him, father ? " Sebastian demanded in excitement. "Yet knowst well, if he lays hands on himself, 't is a mortal sin, and meets an awful doom."

"His doom concerns his Maker, not thee or me or any man, my son. I defend naught. A man should bear his burdens to the end. But there's awful steep climbing in life, jagged paths along the brink, dizzy moments when the heart faints, the head gets wild. No helping hand is near. I say, I'm sorry for such a one, that's all. But I do say it."

"Dost hear, Sebastian? Father and I are sorry for the man," and Vroni confronted her brother aggressively. "But thou, father, say, — is it true his soul's a-flying up from the lowlands on the great wind to-night?"

Dionysius turned toward the dresser where Agathe stood arranging dishes and plates. "I pray thee, wife, take it not amiss, but if on every high wind that blows on the Rough Alp a suicide's soul should fly up to us from the lowlands, surely there would be only distraught folk down below in the valleys and great towns, naught but self-murderers, yet never, indeed, enough for the wind business; for when have we — in the wisdom of providence — a dearth of gales?"

"There, mother, hast heard now!" laughed Vroni, boisterously, from her coign of vantage.

"Put thy shawl over thy head, magpie, and come along with me, and hold the lantern a bit while I speak a good word to them that have a deal more sense than dull human folk," returned the woman, gruffly, striding out and slamming the door, not exclusively because of the tempest. Firm and strong-footed, she tramped toward the barn, while slight Vroni, struggling along in front with the lantern, was blown madly hither and thither, and arrived drenched and breathless.

"Ugh!" she exclaimed, shaking herself vigorously. "The water is trickling down the spine of my back, and I'm as poodle wet as when I plumped into the brook. Wast scolding bravely, mother, eh? Yet not a word heard I, for the blast and the great shrieking and the many voices. And all for a mooly cow that's fed and housed, and can spy no witch at all, and no soul flying, since my father says there be none!"

"Wouldst teach me my business?" came harshly from behind, together with a dive toward Vroni's ear; but that was a wary member; the lantern described a fine swift parabola in the dark barn; and the child giggled from a corner.

"Hush thy cackle: come hither and see that thou hast sense with thy light. Poor Brindle! Wast uneasy? Wast afraid?"

The woman's voice was compassionate; her whole being softened as she passed into the cow's stall and fondled the animal that turned to her with ears outstretched, licked her dress and hands with its rough tongue, and thrust its nose under her arm. Agathe leaned largely against it, extended her arms widely upon it in protection and comfort, stroked it, talked steadily, now in an inaudible murmur, now in low words.

Vroni climbed into the manger of a vacant stall, and, crouching, held the lantern high, and sent its shaft of light straight down upon the strong woman's face in the red kerchief, and upon the cow's curved horns, great shining eyes, and the white spot on its forehead. Beyond, the corners of the barn were black. The storm howled and shook the great doors on their creaking hinges. There was a warm smell of cow, a dry smell of hay and herbs. Agathe continued to reason, plead, and gently to expostulate, lavishing upon the brindle expansive familiarity of caress and confident appeals to its intelligence. The child's impish smile vanished. Mute, intent, grave-eyed, she watched her mother and listened to the onslaught of the wind.

"Was not the heather blessed on the Feast of the Assumption? Did I not pluck it myself, and take a big armful to church for the blessing, and hang a bunch on the door and one under the eaves and one over my brindle's stall? Naught shall harm thee. Evil is on the wind. When it passes, be thou still, my brindle. Make not the smallest sound. Dost hear me? Dost mark well? Stir not. Quiet with hoofs and tail. Lift not thy white nose once and moo. Art wise? Art calm?"

With large lingering hands, Agathe took farewell of the animal, that merely turned its soft eyes and gleaming white spot after her, but whatever its private reflections, made no protest at being left alone.

Preceded now by a tolerably docile torchbearer, Agathe completed her rounds by briefly introducing her reassuring presence into the apartments of her calves, pigs, and hens, whose not over-sensitive organizations seemed in truth curiously roused, restless, apprehensive, and

singular of behavior. With each species she
had her eminently successful method of approach. Each after its kind gave ample response. All animals became, as it were,
humanized under her influence. None could
resist her sympathetic affection, her insight,
her deferential tribute to its higher nature.
When she had laid magnetic hands upon them,
conversed with them fraternally, they too sub-
sided into their wonted nocturnal tranquillity;
and mother and daughter once more braved
the perilous passage of the barnyard, where
Vroni staggered with head bent low beneath
the blinding rain, and the tempest strove to lift
her off her feet.

"Oho!" she called lustily. "A shove,
mother, just a good hand up, and I'll mount
and ride this runaway wind, and be myself a
live, live witch — the only sort there is — 'tis
my father says it!"

Nixy-like she sprang across the threshold,
rivulets and pools marking her course. Shooting a volley of wayward smiles at the weaver,
she energetically wrung her short skirts, rubbed
her wet throat, hair, and glowing face, scourged
herself smartly from head to foot, and stopped
abruptly to cry: —

"Thou, mother! Wouldst like me better had I two little horns up here?" Wagging impudent fingers right and left from her forehead, where her charming hair lay wet in rings, she thrust forward her long throat and grinned like a demon of race.

"Maybe, hadst thou below them a gentle jaw and not thy clapper-tongue. Art coming, Mann? 'Tis after eight, and time the light was out. Though thou be stiff-necked and believest not, on such a night 'tis best we say our prayers and sleep. Besides, why sit about and burn good oil?"

Moving briskly to and fro, still keenly on the trail of things to put to rights, she cast ungracious glances upon the three men smoking their long pipes, and spoke with her characteristic high-pitched and resonant discontent.

Sebastian, ever intent upon holiness, was pouring over the Catechism; while Melchior idly turned the well-thumbed leaves of the only other available literature, — the almanac. Presently Sebastian groaned with vehemence.

"Hast stomach-ache?" bluntly demanded Agathe.

Unheeding her allusion to his base body

3

born in sin, trembling rather for the safety of his father's immortal soul, Sebastian stammered : —

"Didst do that, father?"

"I did, my son," said the weaver, tranquilly.

"'T is a sin, father!"

"Not so, my son. No sin, at least I trust 't is none."

"Bestir thyself, Sebastian. Melchior, when tasks be done, 't is time to sleep. Wast ever owl-like, Mann. Teachest thy sons to turn night into day. Dost think the good Lord made the dark that men might loll with pipes and stretch long lazy legs and argufy?"

"I'll but finish this little job of tinkering of odds and ends. 'T will not take long."

"I'll go to rest then first for once," she returned morosely, "being weary and wet to my bones. See that ye three have sense to follow, and mind the fire and light. The girl is gone. A wonder I had not to drive her! Good-night," she muttered curtly, and went.

"How couldst thou, father?" exclaimed Sebastian, his emotion but augmented by suppression.

Vroni, delighted with herself, rose from the

shadow where she had crouched behind her father's chair.

"Art too large for sly tricks," he said coldly.

"Ah, father, little father," she wheedled.

"Go. Knowst I like not cheating ways. Nor canst thou say thou learnst such from thy mother, who is open and straight as daylight."

"Take it not ill," she faltered, drooping under his rare rebuke.

"Go," he returned, unrelenting. "Yet, stay. Art wet still and chilled. Warm thyself a bit. There's still some heat."

"Father!" she pleaded, for he was looking above and around her head. "*Väterchen!*"

"Art my Mädel?" he smiled his good smile. "Knowst without words what I cannot abide. 'Tis enough said. Warm thyself and go to thy bed."

Small, demure, and unobtrusive, she took her knitting and sat down in the chimney corner by the stove,—a poor thing minus rings or covers,—where a few fagots still burned dully, puffing smoke and soot into the room.

With gloomy mien, and as from a swollen throat, the dark Sebastian resumed:—

"I wait still for thy answer. How couldst thou do it, father? Why?"

" Because I must needs remember the others,
my son," the weaver declared firmly, — " the
others all round the round world, and all the
others still that lived and died before my
time."

Sebastian, his big-jointed and zealous index-
finger boring a certain obnoxious spot on the
small page open on the table, began in a loud
voice to expound.

Now Dionysius the weaver, in reflective, un-
controversial mood, and merely in accordance
with the gentle trend of his personal convictions, had chanced one day mildly to modify a
statement in the Catechism to the effect that
the Catholic Church is the one and exclusive
" ark of salvation." He had drawn a faint,
pensively wavering, almost imperceptible, but
to Sebastian's mind deadly heretical and abominable, pencil-mark through the word *only*.

Sebastian fumed, shook, sawed the air,
pounded the table with his fist, and fairly
wept, in what would have been a diabolical
temper had the subject under debate been
mundane. Melchior, privately agreeing that
it was an impious pencil-stroke, deemed it discreet to mutter something unintelligible, and
sneak off unobserved. Vroni stole to her

father's side, her knitting needles clicking nervously; greedily drank in every word, and, if she understood or not, alternately scowled antagonism at Sebastian, and flashed allegiance and devotion upon the weaver, for that potent and precious old reason, — as constraining for the little peasant maid as for the great Montaigne.

Whether, indeed, evil things astride the winds did the mischief that fateful night, or whether the ill-starred pencil-mark, long lurking in the book, popped into view and imprinted itself the more indelibly upon Sebastian's irascible soul, because of the unwonted absence of the strong tutelary deity who brooked in that kitchen none other wrath but her own, both men grew perfervid.

The weaver began, it is true, with an indulgent smile, and was able for some time to parry his son's thrusts with composure. But nothing rouses the old Adam in the best of us quicker than a religious tussle. Besides, Sebastian's was a pre-eminently contagious choler. Then these were father and son; and what is more truly exasperating than to discover our nearest and dearest presuming to differ from us a hairsbreadth in the views

which we, for our part, know to be conducive
to eternal peace?

So they wandered on over the world's hot-
test battle-ground, stopped now and again for
a good hearty set-to, and finally — oh, luckless
wights! — rushed upon the vexed question of
papal infallibility: Dionysius asserting His
Holiness only in his function as Saint Peter's
successor was infallible that the teachings of
the Church might form one unbroken, perfect
chain; while Sebastian, frantically, incoher-
ently, and with the roaring oratory of a bull of
Bashan, tossed, trampled, and tore to shreds
the theory of merely academic infallibility, and
insisted the Pope was also as mortal man, in
word, deed, and the secret recesses of his heart,
flawless and impeccable.

Not dialectic Andover, no solemn synod
sitting upon a recalcitrant brother who had
avowed himself not sound on hell-fire and
tottering over infant baptism, not High and
Low Churchman in full tilt, not even Dun
Scotus and Albertus Magnus were ever more
thrilled with intolerance, more spurred by
theological acerbity, more doughty in disputa-
tion, more persuaded of the supreme importance of unhorsing the antagonist, than

were this pair of peasants of the Rough
Alp.

They heeded neither shrieking wind nor
lapse of time. It is significant that at a
tolerably early stage of the argument they
forgot to refill their pipes. To the child
who, deft and unobtrusive, exceptionally a
wise virgin, replenished now oil, now wick,
they deigned no glance. Nothing indeed
could better have suited her lawlessness than
that her father should for once ignore her
existence. After each silent ministration, she
effaced herself in the shadowy background,
was guiltily glad to be up so late, and slyly
exultant that if indeed the mother's ears were
still open, the storm must drown all other
sounds.

Vroni heard the angry night booming at
sturdy wall, at roof and clattering casement
— drenching, battering, howling, — retreating
but to return with ever fiercer torrents and
more evil gusts; heard the contentious vibrations of the men's deep voices hurling at each
other great words about Almighty God and
Holy Church; heard, in spite of herself, amid
the tumult within and without, the ghastly
train of which her mother told, — black witches

and damned souls. To the young, over-excited brain the phantom cavalcade seemed often very real and near, although she chid herself, and knew there were none such, for 't was her father said it.

At length, Sebastian clutched his shirt as if suffocating, rushed from the house, and, so torrid was his religious fervor, would not cross its threshold for a whole year, thereby sorely grieving the kindly soul of Dionysius the weaver.

Doubtless one result of his mild and meditative apostasy was that Sebastian ultimately left Hexenfels and obtained a — to his mind — quasi-sacerdotal situation as steward of the great Swiss Convent of St. Scholastika, where he not only did excellent service in the care and direction of farms, vineyards, cattle, serving men and maids, but plucked brands from the burning to his heart's content, dispensed anathemas to erring fellow-creatures with splendid prodigality of measurement and a distinctly hierarchical relish, and enjoyed all his days a reputation for eminent sanctity.

But when on that witch-night he strode wrathfully into the storm, his father sprang up quickly, ran after him, called, returned, waited a while at the open door, and shook his head, incredulous and much perturbed.

"I went too far," he muttered. "That I could go so far!" He stood tall in his gray drilling and leather apron, and stretched his legs a bit, an unwonted flush on his face, his thoughts remote. Suddenly he laughed, walked over to the cupboard and tossed down a mug of cider at one draught, and Vroni marvelled, for this was never his way.

"Ei, ei! Thou here? Art crazy, child? Or rather hast a crazy father to forget thee. How will the mother chide! With reason too. And my poor Bastel fleeing like Cain. Ei, ei! Dost think he'll stop at Tante Ursula's? Will Marie wake and take him in?"

She shrugged her shoulders.

"He? What matters it? His temper boils and splutters so 't will keep him warm enough. I think he'll run on like the clock, till he runs down."

"He may be peppery, but he's good as gold. 'T was I that went too far. 'T was my fault. I rasped him sorely, yet knew he could not bear it. Come, come, child, make haste. Strange thou 'rt not heavy with sleep. Art bright-eyed still and hast hot cheeks."

"Thou, too, *Väterchen!*" she retorted with a laugh, "art all alive. Thine was brave talk. Never heard I the like. Could listen till sunrise."

" 'T was naught, 't was naught," he replied, his face alert and full of light.

"*Ach!* I doubt Father Aloysius could talk so big and full mouthed!"

"Nay, child, 't is far removed from what thou meanest. 'T is echoes only. But it calls back old days when I was young. And though 't was wrong to rasp Sebastian, I fear me I took my pleasure in it!" he admitted in a queer, half-exultant, half-shamefaced way to his little comrade, who, sparkling and eager, nodded with curiously sympathetic recognition of his mood, and a keen search to discover what his mind was beholding beyond the horizon of her small experience.

" 'T was fine in the old days, father? Lov'st them well. 'T is in thy face."

"Seest, Mädel, shouldst hear what I once used to hear. Men with booklearning in their pates, and ready wits and bold, — fearing naught. 'T is like that in the great world. There too knew I a strange and troublous time in which I was driven wildly,

and had not ever a fair reckoning — of which,
when thou art older, thou and I will one day
speak. Then the music!"

He sighed, looking off thoughtful and
absent again.

"Art missing for something, father?" she
asked, wistful, in instant reflection of his
changing mood.

"Nay, I'm old and staid now, and — having thee — content. I but remembered."

She came close and leaned her cheek against
his arm.

"Yet art ofttimes missing for something
with thine eyes."

For some moments he was silent.

"Seest, little one," he said low, smiling
down upon her with great sweetness, "'t is
like this. The good thoughts we once get
hold of we can always keep stored in our
heads, and quietly take them down one by one
as we need them, and turn them over and put
them back, and disturb nobody. But the
great music. If a man has once heard it, it
follows, yet floats off; he cannot seize and
hold it — and so, 't is true, many a time I'm
missing for it. 'T is a sort of hunger in the
heart."

III

At fifteen, Vroni was fairly tall, slight, and
of compact build, her brown face a small oval
on a slender throat, her mouth eager and red.
Every morning she parted her hair smoothly,
brushed it straight, meek, and flat on either
side her head, — as did every other girl who
respected herself in the whole region, — and
braided it in a long tail as thick as a man's
fist. But before night all meekness had fled
before the waves and curls that broke loose
mutinously as the shining tail went frisking
and flaunting, catching and dispensing sunlight wherever it swung. Even in Hexenfels,
where the sterility of the soil effectually pre-
cluded overmuch attention to mere beauty
in woman, the Distel-Bauer, old as well as
young, — Blasius, Sepp the joiner, Jokel,
Hans, Jörg, and Michel, in fact, all the men
were moved to turn and stare after her as she
passed, and to say one to another: —

"The weaver's Vroni is a tidy maid."

About this time Dionysius, on a sudden, began to start up from his loom in working hours, — a proceeding which, the aggrieved Agathe clamored, was without precedent in heaven or on earth. Naught that concerned his daughter escaped his quiet observation: where she was working every hour and with whom, the unanimity of men's eyes at church, young Blasius and Sepp ever impending, and Michel hanging about at a discomfited distance, when he himself intervened for the walk home in the twilight.

He knew well that she never gave one of the lurking swains so much as a friendly glance, rarely enough a decent word, but wide and malicious stares in plenty, and laughter of a frankly explosive sort. Yet she felt his gaze resting ever more thoughtfully upon her. He would often lay his hand on her head and look straight in her eyes, long, searchingly, troubled, one might almost have fancied regretfully — although they were bewitching eyes of the brown that is touched with fitful yellow gleams. He was chiefly wishing, among many other things, that she was, well — less Vroni-ish.

"Better bind thy wild hair about thy head

tight and modest," he said one day, frowning, and she did it; but as for Sepp, Hans, Jörg, Michel, and the rest, not a man of them stared less, — rather more.

The outward resemblance between father and child was becoming even more pronounced.

"Strange thou shouldst be more like me than all my sons — without, and alas, sometimes I fear, within!"

"Dost wish I were a boy? Wouldst like me better?" she returned blithely.

"Nay, Vroni. Thou art my heart's child. But the world is easier for the lads."

"Shame, father, wouldst have another growling Sebastian or long-legged, sheep-faced Melchior instead of thy Mädel."

Even his peculiar headaches she was beginning to develop, not too frequently, yet when they came, so blinding, crushing, and maddening, she would fiercely beat her head against the wall; and when they went, they would leave her wilder than ever, — uncontrollable in mirth and recklessness.

"My child, *mein Herzenskind*," murmured Dionysius, in deep distress and strange contrition, when he first found her on her bed quite desperate with pain, "have I then given

thee that accursed inheritance?" and, Agathe's
great voice resounding reassuringly from the
second field, he took her in his arms and
rocked her to and fro, and two tears not her
own fell on the young girl's cheek.

In those days Agathe was continually harp-
ing on one strain. The girl should bestir
herself, see the world, and earn some money
like her sisters before her.

"Not yet," the weaver would reply frowning. "Art possessed, wife, to get rid of her,
— and she but over young."

"Yet understands her work when once at it
better than those twice her age. What shall
the great girl do here? Do I perchance need
her? Am I not woman enough for my own
business and thrice as much more?" she demanded jealously. "Shall she laze about and
eat us out of house and home, and times so
hard? Is she then other flesh and blood than
her sisters, who took their turn and went down
to the lowlands? Fie, Mann! Wouldst keep
the wind and rain from her if thou couldst!
Wast ever foolish over the maid! But by
good luck she hath a mother who hath taught
her to work, as no flighty little maid ever
worked before, and no thanks to thee, Mann!"

Agathe was right. Where diligence was
for all imperative, no girl worked so well or
so joyously as Vroni. Impetuous, swift of
movement and speech, full of frolic as a
kitten, she was clever at whatever she undertook. Nothing was a hardship. Nothing
daunted her. Not even when she and the
long file of men and women toiled painfully
up the ledge impassable for carts, and balanced
upon their heads great baskets of manure to
fertilize their stony potato fields. This arduous climbing partook indeed of the nature
of an inexorable sacred rite, a sacrifice to the
austere spirits of the soil, for Hexenfels sub-
sisted chiefly upon the humble potato.

The Lindls drank coffee only upon Sunday
mornings. On week-days, they had for breakfast potato-soup, or a thickened milk soup,
or a porridge made of dried oats. At noon,
Spatzen — a sort of home-made vermicelli —
or flour dumplings with fresh salad, or a dish
of potatoes mixed with radishes. For supper,
thick sour milk and potatoes boiled in their
jackets, — all the year round and in every
house in the village. Beside this, they partook of *Vesper*, or luncheon, regularly at
eleven and four, always a bit of black bread

and a glass of cider. More opulent families in Hexenfels drank beer for *Vesper;* poorer, an amazing beverage called *Cibeben-Most,* which although brewed of naught but the innocuous dried currant of commerce and soft spring water, like many another marriage of elements mild but incompatible, fermented into unearthly sourness. Of meat they partook seldom, and never bought it. When they killed a calf or pig or kid, they distributed portions among neighbors who in their turn responded with like courtesies.

The Lindls, according to the Hexenfels scale of measurement, possessed neither poverty nor riches. They kept ordinarily two cows; when there was dearth of fodder only one, but always two calves, and usually a couple of goats. Every family, even the poorest, had a cat; only well-to-do people — herein lay a fine distinction — a dog. Dionysius had none.

To have six children and be well-to-do on the Rough Alp would have been indeed a marvellous achievement. It is fair to say Dionysius the weaver never so much as attempted it. Like his neighbors, he had inherited his land covered, so to speak, knee-

deep with mortgages. These were veritable
heirlooms handed along with the wretched
little farms from generation to generation.
Nobody ever thought of making the feeblest
attempt to extricate himself. If by chance
a small legacy or other windfall surprised a
man, he straightway bought an extra cow, or
another field — to be mortgaged, as is obvious,
in due time. Hence, if for no other reason,
money was never what is euphemistically
called on the Stock Exchange "easy" or even
"firm." People there mostly did without
it, and year in year out got along fairly
well.

Fuel fortunately was not dear. Magnifi-
cent forests clothed the slopes below them.
Here, at intervals, lordly cavaliers with long-
legged boots, guns, dogs, and men in livery,
intruded upon the great stillness their alien
shouts and jollity, and the sad havoc which
they called sport; and here one fixed day in
every month the humble poor of Hexenfels
were permitted, with fitting injunction and
warning, and under due surveillance of the
forester on guard, to file in and fetch what
fagots they needed, provided they conducted
themselves meekly as beseemed their station,

and were mindful to break only dry branches and not injure the trees.

The Lindls never availed themselves of this privilege — another fine distinction. But Vroni, trained to utilize everything imaginable, gathered in those woods masses of pine-cones which made the best possible ironing-fire; and in the autumns, but not every year, she would find there quantities of beechnuts, from which she extracted an excellent oil for cooking as well as illuminating purposes. However, even black Anastasia, daughter of rich Anton the brewer, did no less, and such thrifty devices could never compromise the sturdy independence of the family of Dionysius the weaver.

Anton was the village Midas, and took himself seriously, as Midases do usually, and brewers no less. He dearly loved attention to his soft and pompous personality. Once on his fête, or name-day, pert Vroni, a small child then, for a freak left her giggling little mates huddled together at the side of the road, advanced alone, kept her face quite straight, and in the measured accents of her seniors, yet as clear as a bell, gave him the deferential salutation with which all the vil-

lagers without distinction, being but Rough
Alp boors and not educated up to the delicacy of D'yer-do and Ta-ta, accosted one
whom they had not recently seen: —

"God greet thee. Thy health is dear to
me."

So much by way of dignified preliminaries.
Then followed fittingly for the festal day:

" I congratulate. I commend myself."

Much pleased at this ovation, he gave her a
silver groschen. Having cleverly organized
her forces, she and her cronies, a year from
that day, stood bravely in a line and spoke
the congratulatory word in unison. Each received a groschen. The year after, the little
mob was larger, with like results. The next
year the whole school — it was not a stupen-
dous body — marched to the brewer's, and
every rascal of them got a silver groschen
from the highly flattered Anton.

Thus the procession gradually crystallized
into a public institution — an inalienable
privilege of the school-children. Great would
have been the tumult had they found themselves deprived of the *Anton-groschen*, and
the smirking Anton would have sadly missed
this insidious tribute to his popularity — after

all probably as spontaneous and disinterested as most great public demonstrations in honor of the mighty. The creator of the rite was however much perturbed when at length the weaver intimated she should no longer lead the triumphant march of the school to the brewery.

"Art too large, Mädel."

" 'T is *my* groschen, father!" she returned reproachfully.

"So childish still? Wait. I 'll give thee thy groschen. My tall maid surely wants naught of old Anton."

"Keep thy groschen, father. Hast not a pocketful of silver like Anton. Art not fat and foolish either. 'T is not the silver bit — but seest?" — hot tears of vexation in her eyes though she smiled still — " 't is stupid to be always older and pulled up short, now here, now there. Nay, keep thy groschen. The school may go for all of me. Say, father, wouldst really have me slow as Tante Ursula?"

"Nay, Mädel, I 'd have thee thyself, but wiser," he said a little sadly. "Were 't possible, God knows I 'd have thee wise."

In truth he had, in spite of his great love,

small mercy on the girl. When the yearly
market or *Kirchweih* came, or carnival time
briefly stirred the staid folk to lighter, freer
movement, or a prospective wedding absorbed
public attention for months, or a christening
or funeral evolved agreeable reunions with
the obligatory consumption of viands — and
all such events were momentous and exciting
in the extreme to young Vroni — full three
days beforehand Dionysius would look careworn, and anxiously begin his exhortations,
instructing, enjoining, and warning in such
wise that the girl, glowing with anticipation,
would protest mischievously : —

    " 'T is terrible to hear thee, father, and fairly
spoils the taste for frolic. Surely 't were
best I stayed at home and twirled my thumbs
and held my breath to please thee."

    But even his overweening solicitude had to
grant that the few merrymakings harmed her
not a whit. She grew taller and prettier, but
hardly less childlike. He could find no fault
in her. All that she had been, all that she
used to do, she still was and did; but everywhere and always he, pondering much, was
vaguely troubled.

    Regularly on Sundays, toward evening, she

walked as when a child with her girl friends
in the fields and woods, sang folksongs,
plucked forget-me-nots, laughed riotously,
and when he came for her ran swiftly to meet
him, — on her face the look he thought the
most beautiful thing on earth, clung to him,
strolled with him, and seemed as blithe, unconscious, and innocently unruly as ever. In
her was indeed no alarming change. But his
heart was never at rest, for he saw Sepp, Jörg,
and Blasius sitting on the stile, their short
loose Sunday jackets of brand-new blue cloth,
in each hat a red carnation, and knotted
attractively under each chin between the corners of the unbleached shirt collar, a flaming
silk handkerchief.

The weaver, like most of his race and kind,
greatly loved their quietly commemorative
family fêtes and simple gala days, which,
however barren their symbols, were yet informed and spiritualized by the dignity of
gentle observance. On Agathe's birthday, or
rather name-day, she always received a pound
of loaf-sugar, and, according to ancient custom,
a great wreath of wild flowers, which Vroni
plucked, bound, and hung by her mother's
bed.

As school-child, Vroni had also to learn
and repeat each year, in honor of the festival,
a text or hymn. On her father's name-day
she presented him too with a wreath, and
spoke her little verse; while from Agathe
he received undeviatingly six *pfennigsworth*
of snuff — "*Doppel Mops* and Fine Merino
mixed " — and Backstein cheese for an equal
amount. On Vroni's *fête* she was usually presented with a new kerchief, an apron, and some
apples. Now that she was so old, her kerchief
was of apple-green silk and had a fringe.

Were the gifts mean, they yet caused honest pleasure. Diamonds have been known
to fail to do as much. Were the festal days
celebrated beneath an obscure peasant weaver's
roof, they were ushered in with essentially
respectful rites and attended from dawn till
eve with honors. One wore one's Sunday
clothes. Exceptional deference and tranquillity pervaded one's home atmosphere. In
the village, everybody one met extended a
cordial hand and said impressively: *Ich gratu-
lire;* while relatives and friends made a special pilgrimage across one's threshold to utter
the same felicitation. The fact of one's existence was thus agreeably accentuated, its

importance in creation — often regarded skeptically — now made manifest. A beneficent dimness enveloped the sad train of cares, fears, misfortunes, sorrows, blunders, and infirmities always dogging one's heels. One thanked God for what one had, and stopped bewailing what one had not.

By inheritance, tradition, and natural tendency this, more or less, was the attitude of the weaver's gentle spirit toward these simple gala days. These too now suffered a change. Vroni duly made her wreaths and spoke her verses as carefully and innocently as of old. But on Frau Agathe's name-day — an event hitherto wholly unnoticed by the youth of the village — a pot of lard, brought a long distance, was significantly laid at her feet by big Jörg, while Blasius, blushing, but sustained by the consciousness of munificence and patrimony, appeared with no less than a sugar-loaf under his arm. Dionysius, in his turn, was distinguished at the hands of Michel and others by choice portions of newly slaughtered animals. Over all offerings to her larder Agathe chuckled, Dionysius looked disturbed; Vroni mocking or indifferent and remote.

On a May day, when the eligible bachelor-

dom of Hexenfels had the privilege of inti-
mating preference and secret hopes, a young
beech and two young birches were planted in
the night before Vroni's casement.

"Shall I chop them down, father?" she
asked disdainfully.

"Nay, child. Let them be. Things must
take their course," he answered slowly.

"At this rate we'll soon have a young wood
round us, — and before long a wedding, I make
no doubt," remarked Agathe, well pleased.
"Seest, Mann? There's many a richer, but
Vroni, the lads all know, hath a right sort of
mother, and is a tidy worker. She hath but
to choose."

"My little maid!" sighed the weaver, and
laid his hand on her head.

"Thou, Vroni! What thinkest thou? Was
it Sepp, Blasius, and long Jörg? Blasius for
sure, eh? An orderly lad, Blasius, and brought
me a four-mark sugar-loaf. Planting trees
costs nothing, but not all do bring sugar. To
be sure old Blasius has his eye on the thick
Anastasia; yet he likes thee well enough, and
looks after thee when thou springst about,
and wert thou but a little decent spoken to
him, and less wild and unmannerly, he'd not

mind that thou hast not her stocking full of money. At least he'd get over it. And there's not so good a place for a wife in all Hexenfels, mind that, with the mother dead and out of the way, and nobody to hinder, and the two men a decent sort, and the good fields and good cattle, and money to spare. Art getting on in years, Vroni. 'T is time to cease springing and shouting like mad. 'T is time to think sense."

"Dost call Blasius sense?" laughed Vroni. "Nay, not he! Was ever a dunce at school, mother, and, oh, his little eyes, and, oh, his big ears, and, oh, how he stuttered and shuffled and shambled, the sugar-loaf under his arm, and his nose redder than his hair or his new rainbow cravat. I could but stare and wonder which thing did set the other a-fire where all was blazing — but 't was his nose for sure."

"A man's nose is no disgrace, and has naught to do with marriage," proclaimed Agathe. "Anastasia will ne'er spy the bit of red. For my part, I marked it not at all for the good sugar-loaf."

"Black Anastasia is two and twenty. 'T is old. Let her take her stocking and go and marry Blasius. As for me, though the men

plant trees as high as the Tooth, I like none
but my father."

"Vain talk, empty. as a puff-ball. 'T is true
he spoils thee with his notions."

Vroni, a little scornful, yet in high good
humor, retorted smiling: —

"Leave me yet in peace, mother, with thy
talk of weddings. Seest well I am not ready.
I but laugh at them. For my life I cannot
help laughing at the men. Why should they
bother me? Do I bother them? Do I so
much as look at them, except they stand heavy
in my path?"

"Because thou art ill-mannered and wild as
no other, except it be a hawk. Must marry
sooner or later, eh?"

"Why?" demanded Vroni, sturdily.

"Hear her!" and Agathe raised protesting
eyes and hands toward heaven.

"Yes, why — if I want no man?"

"For what did God make maids except to
marry?"

"Where did He say that? Whom did He
tell it?" demanded the girl, a wicked light in
her eyes.

"Art not seemly, Veronika. So speaketh
no good, pious maid."

"Tante Ursula is pious beyond all women far and near, yet never married."

"She had her father's house to keep, and enough to live on. She is different."

"Oh! then I, too, will be different. I will work and earn money that I need never marry. And when thou diest, — take it not amiss, mother! — I'll be like Tante Ursula and keep house for my father."

"Art wilder than a boy and bolder with thy tongue. But though over-mirthful, marriage will tame thee yet. Wait!"

"Hast taken the best man thyself, mother. Mightst well have left me my father!"

"'T is empty talk enough, I say. Go now about thy business."

"'T is no use, mother. Canst not make me other than I am. I'll like no man for trees or sugar-loaves. Seest, until one comes along with my father's eyes and smile and way of speech, and notions, mother, all his notions, and his good heart, and his hand on my head, I'll like no man. Hast heard now, mother!" and as she went she sang loud and sweet:

> "*Mein Schatz ist ein Weber,*
> *Ein Weber ist er.*"

"My little maid!" said the weaver once more, smiling, straightening himself free and relieved.

"Hast wholly spoiled the girl, seest? Canst smile? Fie!"

"I like her thus," Dionysius said simply. "I would not have her casting sly eyes at men. My Mädel pleases me. What's amiss, wife? Is but a child."

"Child here, child there! Art losing thy good wits? Yet dost mark she is a maid like another, and the men's eyes ever on her. If she stays here, she'll marry speedily, and where's the harm, say I, though thou knittest thy brows like a thundercloud. If she goes away, she'll earn some money for us, which is better still — and marry all the same, but later. Mark my words. Whether so or so, she'll marry, and though she stare cool with her big eyes to-day, to-morrow she may hang her head and turn red or white in the cheek."

"She's over-young to marry," muttered the weaver, disturbed.

"Then send her off to work."

"She's over-wild and innocent-like to go among strangers."

"They'll tame her, I take it. But keep her here, an thou willst, and marry her straightway. Why not? As for me," she trumpeted, " I 'm reasonable! "

"I fain would see her happy," Dionysius replied wistfully.

"Happy! Mann, art enough to provoke a saint."

"I seek not to provoke thee. I would but show thee my thought, for the child's sake. Let us for once consult quietly together, for she is our child, thine as mine."

"*Herr Je!* Art rarely civil! Mostly 't is as if thou thyself hadst plucked her readymade from a fairy bush, or as if she 'd fallen from the sky into thy arms and no trouble to nobody, like roast pigeons into the mouths of the rich! "

"Thou art her mother, and this is my thought," he went on quietly. "There 's rare good stuff in her, but she is not like the others, wife, — take it not ill. She is fiercerhearted, hath more nerve in her joy, would grieve worse if grief came. 'T is dead weary work to plod on side by side with one who understands thee not, and hath no part in thy thoughts. At least I mean I fear 't would be

thus for our girl. Besides, I shall not always
be near her. One does not know these things,"
he said deprecatingly; "but I 'm thinking many
a time I 'm not over-strong. Somehow — not
that they 're not orderly lads enough — I cannot seem to put my mind on one quite fit to
lead my Mädel home."

" 'T is always the same old story and pure
vexation to talk with thee. Naught is good
enough for thy daughter, and thou art no
better than the dog in the manger."

" I know, I know," he returned conciliatingly.
" It maybe I 'm over soft about the little maid.
Have patience, Agathe. I will turn all these
things over in my mind."

" And if thou turnst and turnst till dooms-
day, willst find naught else but a wedding or
the lowlands."

Thus it came about that after a long drought
and an appalling failure of crops, when fodder
and money were scarce, and Dionysius' weaving often interrupted by brief illnesses, when
Blasius, Sepp, Michel, Jokel, Jörg, and Hans
loomed ever more ominous on the near horizon,
and Agathe's contentious voice ceased not its
arguments and vehement reproach, the weaver,
dreary and desperate, resolved to brave the ills

he knew not rather than longer face those he knew too well. Accordingly Vroni, nothing loath and nearly seventeen, left the Rough Alp for the first time, and, commended to the care of a Hexenfels underhouse-keeper, was sent down to the lowlands to Waldmohr Schloss.

5

IV

THREE days and three nights Vroni wept
stormily for home-sickness and acute longing for Dionysius the weaver.   For nearly
three days more she had her headache.
Moreover she missed her mountain winds,
and complained there was no air to breathe.
The housekeeper said it was ridiculous the fuss
the highland girls always made over their
heathenish rocks where no goat could laugh
and grow fat.   But the under-housekeeper,
who still retained a sneaking fondness for
her native village, soothed her ruffled superior on the one side and unreasonable
Vroni on the other, and fortunately it was
not a busy time at the castle, for the count
and countess were gone to town for a court
dinner and a series of family festivities.

Her successive tornadoes left Vroni less
pretty perhaps than ever before in her life,
yet far prettier than most people one sees, —
which is perhaps not saying much; certainly

than anybody in Schloss Waldmohr, not ex-
cluding the countess herself — as still, straight,
and not a little gloomy, she followed the under-
housekeeper one morning into the great
kitchen where were assembled smart maids
and lackeys in agreeable dalliance.

She hardly looked at them, was wholly
undazzled by the Schloss and its contents.
Things were bigger, brighter, and different
from what she had known; that was all. A
group of Arab Sheiks suddenly transported
to a European capital, amazed observers not
only by their measureless tact, their subterra-
nean wisdom and angelic courtesy, but by their
utter indifference to much of the complicated
machinery which civilization deems of over-
whelming importance. So, too, was Vroni.
The untutored mind has its own dignity.

But when a large, dark, clean-shaved man
with a white cap on his head passed her corner, she took him for a person of importance
— which he emphatically was — and instinctively made her quick reverence as when she met
Father Aloysius, or when suddenly on one of
her beechnut or snail expeditions the gay
hunting gentlemen flashed upon her in the
dense wood. The smart maids giggled and

jeered; but the French cook, perfectly aware
that he was a great man, deigned not unnaturally to approve her innocent homage; liked
the girl's start of surprise, her flush, her spirited
silence as she faced the gigglers; liked her
defiance and what in a lady of high degree
would be called her sheer haughtiness; liked
her beauty — in short liked her altogether, and
in a twinkling sent forked French oaths and
terrifically rolling r's shooting and crashing
about that kitchen over the heads of that
canaill-l-l-l-le, until their flippant wit was
drenched, and they remembered pressing
duties elsewhere. The Paris chef, like a
great Bourbon in exile, was merely bid-
ing his time. His large emoluments could
ill console him for his sojourn among bar-
barians. He deplored the love of change,
the roving disposition, chagrin at losing a
position to which he had aspired, artistic
temperament — call it what one would —
that had led him to these outskirts of civilization where he was subjected to great and
peculiar tribulations.

Twice a week the chef disdained not to
drive to market and stock his larder. But
even he himself could not foresee his dizzy

flights of intellect, hence something was continually wanting. When an inspiration of his creative genius required a leaf, a mere breath of rare spice, an all-important nothing, he was obliged to send a groom galloping to the nearest market town. On a swift horse this could be done in two hours. Two hours back made four. An hour allowed ostensibly for searching for the object and letting the animal rest, but in reality spent in gossiping and guzzling vile beer, made five, usually nearer six. A pause of six hours on the brink of creation! Had they tied the hands of Michel Ange so long whenever the giant spirit strove to reveal itself, where now were his great works! Did the imbeciles suppose a genius could *réchauffer* ideas like veal? Besides, whatever the object desired, the groom usually failed to fetch it. Either the God-forsaken land produced it not, or the idiot had not comprehended. What a country! What privations!

He was an alien. So too it seemed to him was the handsome, spirited, glowering little being who had the honor to win his protection at the moment of her entrance into official life at Waldmohr. Although some very fair sort of people were about him, his prejudice and language and theirs formed insurmountable obstacles. Each held the other's speech, manners, and racial traditions to be superfluous and grotesque. Some of the upper maids spoke bad French, which he ironically declined to recognize, and when they dared, they in return sniggered at his broken German. Still in a certain sense he was sovereign lord, and kept them well at a distance, and wronged his amiable disposition by assiduously cultivating surliness to the under-cooks, from whom he jealously guarded his professional secrets. A social, chatty being, he forced himself to be taciturn, imagined that by fraternizing with nobody, he was in some vague way upholding a great country and great art, and until Vroni came was lonely in his grandeur.

Her worldly experience he, at a glance, preceived hardly surpassed a squirrel's, but also that there was nothing limp in her understanding. She would have comprehended a Chinaman had she liked him, and she liked the chef instantly, freely, in good comradeship, neither fearing nor flattering him. Such demeanor is pleasing to liberal monarchs.

Her legitimate position would have been in the outer circles among underlings and

novices. With a wave of his smooth hand
he promoted her. He kept her near him,
gave her small tasks, and observed her critically. Not in vain was she Agathe's daughter. She had sensible hands, swift, steady,
wholesome, and clean-skinned, brown but
never rough. They could almost touch pitch
undefiled. The chef watched them and smiled
astutely.

"It is the hand of the artist — the born
cook," he reflected; and what no threat,
money, or prayer could have enticed from
him, he in time lavished upon her, — the
fine fruits of his experience, his esoteric wisdom. It was his good pleasure, his royal
whim.

"Little do you suspect what I am doing, my
poor child, — how should you!" he would
sometimes exclaim with a queer grimace.
"Never mind! The day will come when
you will comprehend and bless the name
of Armand Gireaud."

However wanting in æsthetic appreciation
of the subtleties of *Perdreaux de Rambouillet*
and *Pains de canetons rouennaise*, Vroni was
practically a delightful pupil of whom her
master was proud. He drilled her soundly

in the fundamental principles of cooking-
ranges; he delivered a whole series of im-
passioned harangues upon awful dinner catas-
trophes resulting from minimal errors in
temperature; he took her to market, and in-
culcated his own refined and astute methods
of selection and purchase. Although these
appertained to a higher education than Rough
Alp philosophy dreamed of, she adopted them
with marvellous receptivity, and he had frequent occasion to chuckle over her audacity
and keenness.

As for head reckoning, it was her specialty.
When grown-ups had fluttered the village
school — the *Schultheiss*, Father Aloysius, or
old Anton — and the wretched Blasius, wishing the floor would open and swallow him,
had stammered that America was an island
surrounded by water and occupied by black
men who ate fat and drove sledges drawn by
reindeer, and big Anastasia could not spell
her word, and sat down sobbing stertorously,
even before the teacher spoke, all the children
had turned their frightened eyes toward little
Vroni Lindl, and knew she would stand up as
bold as a lion and do sums in her head like
lightning, until teacher and grown-ups should

smirk at one another again. So finally she went to market for the chef, thereby relieving him of a loathsome task in this strange land, and the worthy shop people from fiendish objurgations in a foreign tongue. She became his trusty adjutant, his envoy, riding gayly to town on sudden secret missions; and were a thing to be had for money, smiles, mother wit, or insolence, she fetched it with a zealous speed unknown to grooms, and laid it in triumph at her master's feet.

She was the only person he would tolerate in his presence when imagining his vast combinations. She alone stood valiantly by his side when he constructed his master-pieces for festivities. He initiated her into the occult mysteries of sauces, the subtle balminess of creams, advanced her rapidly but thoroughly through a whole arcanum of entrées, and once, when the castle was full of guests, folded his arms superbly and proclaimed in the presence of all his aproned corybants: —

"The salmi of pheasant for lunch will be executed by Mademoiselle Véronique." Vroni, quite unconcerned, "executed" the birds. "It's like her impudence," the envious whispered. Yet she bore her honors

with such nonchalance, was so like a hearty
boy, friendly if not interfered with, but returning evil for evil with startling rapidity
and liberal measure, — none really objected
that she was *persona gratissima* with the chef,
above all when the fact was patent that she
coveted nobody's sweetheart.

How much, how exceedingly much in
divers ways that good chef did for her, neither
she nor Dionysius the weaver ever suspected.
Not only was Gircaud occupying her con-
stantly, keeping her happy and amused, offi-
cially training her brain and hands in the
knowledge of manifold delectable receipts of
which the world is not worthy, and unoffi-
cially exercising her in a curiously disorderly
but quite available method of speaking
French — reversing the orderly and unavail-
able methods of boarding schools, — but he
constituted himself a bristling body-guard
between her and all foolish trifling, coarse
flattery, or even honest love-making, which
on the part of the young fellows employed
at the Schloss would have been in his preju-
diced opinion equally detrimental.

In point of fact, the weaver's Mädel was
chaperoned hardly less solicitously than the

chatelaine's young sister, the charming Comtesse Nelka von Vallade. From early morning until late at night the chef and Vroni were companions at work and in the hours of ease which were that great man's prerogative. With him she strolled contentedly in the vegetable gardens where he wisely kept himself in touch with fair smooth candidates for early favor. With him she walked by the river, and even went to the fair, where he was better dressed and more impressive than the count himself.

Being as yet of a somewhat haughty and unmerciful strain toward youths, and best accustomed to the mature gentleness of her beloved weaver, she took it wholly as a matter of course that a man of forty-five or fifty was her work and play-fellow. It was a queer intimacy, and a queerer jargon that they talked, — her village-dialect, his broken German, and flights of French mostly far above her head.

Sheltered by shrubbery and a great sweet-pea trellis on the edge of the kitchen garden was a pleasant corner frequented by the chef after the engrossing event of his day, dinner. Escaping as early as possible, relegating its

mere final details to his vassals, he loved to
array himself in an elegant costume of *villé-
giature*, and, seated upon his favorite bench,
read his "Petit Journal," smoke cigarettes,
chat with his *élève* — in short, unbend and
strive to forget his greatness and his cares.

From this haunt Vroni could watch strangers
staying at the Schloss and guests of an evening, as they chatted over their coffee on the
veranda, or strolled on the high terrace in
the long summer twilight: pale-colored,
fluffy ladies with fans; black and white
gentlemen with long shining shoes, broad
shining shirt-fronts, and little peaked Bantam
coat tails; blue, red, and yellow men, gay
with gold stripes and buttons. Sometimes,
too, from pantry windows she caught fleeting
glimpses of them riding off, two by two, in the
sunshine, knocking balls about on the grass,
or whirling on wheels. They were always talking very much, she noticed, always terribly
glad to see one another, always smiling and
nodding and sunning themselves, always most
pleasant and polite.

She regarded them without envy, almost without wonder. She accepted them composedly,
as mere facts like the great carved stairway,

the pictures and armor in the hall, the many
lights in the dining-room, and the multitude
of novel observances and ceremonies which
from time to time obtained from her a cool
little stare of reconnoissance and nothing more.

But gradually the living picture framed by
arching trees, the panoramic human group
gently animated in movement and color and
gay in long vista beneath the castle towers,
began to exert upon her a subtle influence and
fascination. It was a sort of *al fresco* theatre,
a puppet show for the weaver's Mädel. From
afar she became familiar with the salient peculiarities of her high-born dolls, their contours,
gestures, and manners, and sitting at ease upon
the grass while Gireaud idly read, she edified
him not a little with her running comments, in
which much downright realism was manifest.
She gave them names too, unflattering, irrev-
erent indeed, yet marvellously appropriate
from her candid and impartial point of view:
a stout brunette baroness being "the black
Anastasia;" a red-nosed major, "old Anton;"
a worn-out beau she cheerfully dubbed "Grandad;" one ancient dame of prehistoric line-
age was "Tante Ursula"; another, fierce of
mien, "Frau Widow Boppel" — she who was

once walled up ; and five golden youths of bluest blood, from some trick of hair, of gait, of awkward adolescence, were respectively "Jörg," "Jokel," "Seppl," "Hans," and "the Distel-Bauer."

This mood passed also. Fixing her clear eyes on those denizens of another world, she would grow silent, busy with novel and vague speculations, and knit her brows.

"Well, Vronette, what is it?" asked the chef one evening. "You look as solemn as a *juge d'instruction.*"

"Are they always like that, M'sieu Armand?"

"Always how?"

"'Lazing about," she replied graphically, but without malice. "Always in Sunday clothes. Always jabbering, all at once, so fast, and so dreadfully glad to see one another. Always so chirpy and clucky."

He looked at her curiously, smiled, and laid aside his paper.

"*Ma foi*, child, what would you have? After all it is but the amiable manner of good society. You would not wish them to quarrel?"

"Does it not tire them? It would tire me. Do they never want to stop and do something else? Is that all they do?"

" But you have seen them riding."

" Riding is sense," she deigned to concede.

" And playing games; and they read a little and dress and pay visits, and dress and dine — as you and I know, Vronette. *Sapristi*, how society eats! How grossly much and with what ignorance! It is enough to make one despair of human progress," he bewailed, quite above poor Vroni's range. Yet, strictly considered, what spoken words are not above or below the level of the listener? Then from the bland depths of ignorance where Vroni sported, she had a startling way of leaping up and seizing an idea. " I gave them *Saumon à la Marguéry* for lunch," he continued gloomily. " Who knew it was a dish for gods? Who will remember? "

" I, M'sieu Armand! " was the gay and unexpected response. " For you explained until you grew red as a turkey-cock, and almost wept because I laughed; and you made me copy it in German, and your *Kauterwelsch*, and yet again clean, in my book. Although I don't know what you mean by gods, — surely only heathen folk have more than one, and they are graven images that cannot eat, —

and though I do not roll my eyes and gasp,
for, after all, 't is but fish in a thick and fussy
sauce, be sure I 'll never forget it, and I 'll do
it next time as well as you yourself, so cheer
up, M'sieu Armand," she airily threw an
imaginary pinch of salt at him with his own
gesture, "I shall remember."

The man, with droll solemnity, rejoined:

"Little savage, you will, I know you will.
It is that which is my consolation. Mistake
not, I cast no pearls before the unworthy.
You sleep now like what 's her name in the
fairy tale. You have no soul like the other
one. But you will arise; you will awaken; you
will find your soul."

"Take it not amiss that I laugh, M'sieu
Armand. I understand not one word of your
speech that runs like olive oil from a two
quart bottle, except that you think I can do
the fussy fish; and that I can, to the twirl of
your fingers. But for my life I cannot help
laughing when you snap your eyes and take
your mouth so full."

"Laugh. *Il faut que la jeunesse se passe.*
Then above the gayety of heart you have the
man's head. You seem a *tête de linotte*, but
nothing escapes you. Am I the man to waste

myself? Do I not sharply observe? When had I to tell you a thing twice?"

"You are so very solemn, M'sieu Armand, somehow it makes me laugh the more." She sat down on the grass, drew up her knees, put her chin in her hands and stared at him, mirth and beauty in her eyes.

"It is an impertinent little Vronette grinning at me and chewing sweet-pea stems, all her nice white teeth but too visible — a *gamine*. I am not talking to her. I am speaking to quite a different person — the Vronette of some years hence."

Involuntarily her nonchalant gaze concentrated itself in sudden intelligence.

"To her I say," he continued earnestly, dropping his bombast, "if she remembers me and my words, the world will never trample her under-foot, for she has something the world wants."

For a moment she looked at him in silent, grave inquiry.

"Bah, 't is but cooking!" she exclaimed with her aggressive incredulity, and began to hum: —

> "*Mein Schatz ist ein Weber,*
> *Ein Weber ist er.*"

6

A shade of despair flitted across his features. He folded his arms repressively across his portly white waistcoat.

"Never mind, Vronette," he said with admirable patience. "You are young. You are from the mountains. You are, as it were, like one of your own goats. It is well. I comprehend. I simply remark, Wait."

"*Wait!* 'T is my mother's word," the girl retorted wickedly. "'T is what she always shouted when coming after me to give me a good one on the ear — but I waited not, M'sieu Armand!"

"*Madame votre mère* has done me a great service," he returned gallantly. "I have to thank her and *monsieur votre père* also for the only pleasure I have known in this sad country — the society of their child. For truly you cheer me much, Vronette. You amuse me."

"And you me, M'sieu Armand, you me," she rejoined with pleasing alacrity. "'T is true I've nearly died of laughter over many, and most perhaps till now over Blasius and Seppl — but never yet did I see anybody quite so droll as you."

He raised his eyebrows, but smiled indulgently.

" *Voyons*, Vronette, now that you are reasonable and no longer shaking from top to toe, let me recount you a little tale. The mood is on me. Who knows? It may not return. Before we part, it is well you hear. The daughter of a colleague is *cordon bleu* in a Danish palace, a woman of the stature of a grenadier, but in her creations, what subtlety, what exquisite sentiment! Well, I was ambitious. I longed to have my only daughter emulate her. Not only because I had no son to inherit my art, my traditions, and my honorable reputation, but because I worship the sex. I adore it. More than that I have faith in it. I am a modern man. I have always believed, given talents and the necessary training and women could rise to great heights even in my difficult profession. Yet what, I ask you, is more prosaic, more uninspired a figure than the average woman cook! A lamentable bungler!

" Many a hot argument upon this theme had I with a friend, a lady's tailor by profession, he declaring for the finest needlework in his province, for things requiring not only precision but delicacy of feeling, he could employ only men. Bows, for instance, — adorable butterfly bows, he insisted,

men fashioned best; while I contended in
lovely woman was an *âme d'élite* that needed
but right conditions to reveal itself. You
follow me, Vronette?"

"Nay, scarce one word in a score, M'sieu,"
she returned blithely. "But that's all right.
I'm comfortable. Go on."

"Well, I named my child Armande, and
took her young, as one takes any *artiste* — for
the *trapèze* — for the violin — I gave myself
all pains. I labored with enthusiasm; but
't was a chagrin — a fatality. She was docile,
ah, yes, she was intelligent; but, *hélas*, she had
not the temperament, she had no touch of
greatness — no fire."

"No fire! Then how could you expect
her to cook," demanded Vroni, with her cool
stare.

"Ah, Vronette, I speak of the ideal fire —
le feu sacré!"

"Don't know it. Is it coal or cokes?"

"That is unimportant. Let us pass on to
facts. I renounced my hope. I perceived my
Armande as cook would never get beyond a
bourgeoise mediocrity. Besides her mother
leaned to bonnets. Armande went into bonnets. She is in bonnets now in the Rue St.

Honoré. I was for some time jealous of those bonnets, and, it may be, unjust, but that is past. Her business name is like yours, Véronique. 'T is a good business name. She has it in large gold and white letters over her door. She has succeeded." In his voice, in spite of its elegiac strain, was a vestige of pride. "Perhaps now, Vronette, you comprehend better my interest, my fervor, and why I train you with the training of the man and the artist. You are, as it were, the resurrection of a lost hope."

"I know when people are good to me," she replied sagely, nodding at him with pretty graciousness over the flowers in her hands. "That much I know."

"'T is enough for to-day, my child. The rest will arrive. For you have the head, the hands, the temperament, and 't is Armand Giraud who is giving the instruction. Wait!" he exclaimed with a large and prophetic gesture.

"As for bonnets," he resumed, after crossing his fine shoes and contemplating the vault of heaven, "I do not, at present, flatly deny the charm of bonnets." He surveyed with benevolent reminiscence the bunch of lilac

and purple sweet-peas Vroni was weaving into
her wreath. "They offer, I concede, a cer
tain field for fancy and fine feeling. Then
they are instructive. My Armande writes she
has invented a shape for the American head.
Scientific researches, it appears, have ascertained the American head possesses neither
reverence nor romance. Evidently it requires
its specific bonnet. Interesting that! They
now construct a sort of phreno-ethnological
capote. What think you, Vronette?"

"Naught of your gibberish, M'sieu Armand,
if you don't mind, and all to myself, that
were my father here I 'd make this wreath for
him, for 't is a posy that he loves."

"I 've fatigued you with my long dis-
course?"

"Nay," she rejoined serenely, "for I 've not
listened overmuch."

"I was merely about to say what I always
tell my daughter, that millinery, in spite of
certain meretricious charms, is but a fickle,
fragile thing, and no great essential art like
mine. After all, one could exist without
bonnets."

"Why, of course," cheerily assented bonnet-
less Vroni. "When you are young, you have

your hair; and when you are old, you wear
your kerchief. But cooks, too," she added
shrewdly after a moment. "The world could
get along without cooks."

"Ingrate!"

"It could eat apples and nuts," she affirmed
stoutly. "I like apples. And potatoes boil
themselves. Then there's milk. Oh, yes,
M'sieu Armand, quite enough to eat without
fussy cooking like ours."

He smiled at the implied co-partner-
ship.

"To be sure it earns good wages," she continued joyously; "I send such a lot home,
and heaps more than if I'd been put with the
scullery-maids instead of with you. Besides
I like to be with you," she said, in her warm
and resolute fashion. "I like you," with a
lovely smile of confidence and affection. "I
like men better than women," she added reflectively. "Men are not so silly as maids
—that is, nice old men. There's my father,
and there's you."

She put her wreath, a good solid one as was
the fashion in Hexenfels, well down on her
forehead, and, rising, took her old place of
observation.

"There 's a new one," she said quickly, "a pink one."   After a moment, "I like her."

The chef got up.

"Ah," nodding approval, "it is the countess's sister, Comtesse Nelka von Vallade. Yes, she is *gentille*."

"I like her," repeated Vroni.

"So soon? Why?"

"Does one know why — soon or late? Red Lisl I did ever like, black Anastasia never; but why I could not tell you for your life."

He reseated himself.

"I heard she was expected to-day on her wheel, with her brothers."

"It must be nice on a wheel — like a witch. Oh, M'sieu Armand, they are jumping, the blue and white brothers.   Ha, I can do that! He need not look so pleased with himself. Now the other brother is going over the same hedge.   He 's smiling too.   Ach, was! 'T is but a baby jump.   Oh, see, she 's running down, the pretty one!   She wants to jump it too.   Of course.   And better than they I make no doubt.   Oh, Weh, oh, Weh! They are shaking fans at her.   They 've stopped her.   An old lady 's got her now, and put her up there in the row of grinny people.   But she does not like it, M'sieu Armand. She cannot bear it."

"I presume not," he replied with a little laugh. "But the Comtesse Nelka von Vallade may not jump hedges."

"When I tell you she could!" she retorted indignantly. "Bah, 't is so easy. Look out, M'sieu Armand!" and over his iron-backed bench she flew.

"I said may not, not cannot," he explained, amiably re-adjusting himself. "I doubt not her capacity, though she be no wildfire. On her horse she may jump it, not on her own two feet."

"Is that sense?" demanded Agathe's daughter.

"That I do not pretend to say, but it is *comme il faut* — it is propriety."

"But she may ride that wheel."

"That is the fashion," he rejoined, amused. "Ah, wild little Vronette, do not look so puzzled! Truly you have much to learn, but even that task may be accomplished with the help of the *bon Dieu*."

Charming and pensive under her heavy wreath of sweet-peas, she still regarded the ladies and gentlemen, and remarked meditatively: —

"They do not earn money and send it home
to their parents?"

"But no— You know that without asking."

"I knew it," she said slowly; "but never
had it in my thoughts.   Then the parents
earn the money?"

"Sometimes the father earns it; sometimes
he has it without earning."

"Oh," she muttered, with a thoughtful air.
"And the pretty Comtesse Nelka, who must not
jump a wee little hedge—her father works for
her?   How does he work?"   Her face grew
soft, for she saw the front room, the loom,
and the dear weaver weaving early and
late.

"Count Vallade is Cabinet-Chef — and
thankless business it is, so far as I know.
He works like a galley slave.   I do not envy
him," observed the other sort of chef, with
fraternal commiseration.   "He's worn to
death with papers and the King and State
affairs, you know."

"Oh, is he?" she murmured, with the same
gravity.   "Does he earn much?"

"Not so very much," he replied, amused
at her persistence.   "Certainly not enough.
For he has heavy expenses and only his salary.

Ma foi, three gay lieutenants are no bagatelle in a man's budget."

"Surely the big grown sons earn their own living!"

"By no means. He has to allow them something every month to eke out their pay."

"The lazy louts! They ought to be ashamed."

"It is but the way of their world," he returned indifferently. "They have to live according to their station, I presume."

"Why?"

"Well, I hear the valets say so. They seem to know. They have it all glib on their tongues. They say the old count is a good sort and terribly hard pressed. They say the young men are high-livers with horses, wines, gaming, and the rest, — Count Benno's pace is the worst of all. They say it's a lucky thing the older daughter, Comtesse Clotilde, got Count Waldmohr, and that the younger is soon to marry that old wreck, Baron von Frege, who is rich as Monte Christo. And they say the sooner young Flemming is out of the way, the better for the Vallade projects, for the young people are sweethearts from the cradle. There you have a whole

feuilleton, Vronette.   Wait, let me see if old
Frege is still there.   He is leaning against
the veranda railing near Comtesse Nelka.
He'd better put on a shawl.   It's getting
damp.   Young Flemming stands on the other
side of her, and won't budge."

"Du, meine Güte!   The yellow cheeked
one with the beak and the whalebone legs!
Grandad!"

"And the wig and the teeth and the cor-
sets.   Yes, that's the sort he is.   And it's
not the worst of him," muttered the French-
man under his moustache.

"Does she want him?" she asked, with even
and long-drawn emphasis.

"Of course not, infant!   Can you not
comprehend?   The brothers living as they
do and must — the father half distracted, the
mother urging on the match!   And Comtesse
Nelka can help no end when once she gets
those millions."

"The witch-faced man will give them to
her, and she will give them to the others?"

"Somewhat, if not precisely so."

"She ought to go to work," said Vroni, in
a clear and rather stern voice.   "It would be
better and more sensible.   In Hexenfels, we

work and help when we are small, but earn no
wages.   When we are grown, our kind earns
wages.   I would no longer want my father to
do all for me as if I were a child," adding,
with fine irony: "'T is true youths plant trees,
and bring fresh pork, and hang about the stile,
and make frog-eyes at one amazingly.   Young
men are prone to do such things.   It is their
foolish nature.   What matters it?   It dis-
turbs nobody.   My mother is for marrying.
My father not.   I take after my father," she
concluded with dignity.

In the girl's mind seemed a sudden awaken-
ing, lurking in her childishness a certain
serious strength and consecutive grasp of
things hitherto unperceived.

"Bravo, Vronette!"

"Why should you laugh?" she asked, a
little nettled.   "I but mean sense.   It is all
quite easy to understand.   If the Comtesse
Nelka would learn to work, she could earn her
own bread.   That would help her father when
he is weary at nightfall, and she need not
marry the man-witch.   As for her three
brothers, — shame on their lazy bones, — she
should give them a piece of her mind."

"Quite true.   Only great people have an-

other way of looking at things. But you
need not glare at me, Vronette. I am not
responsible for their *bêtises*. I merely fill my
place," he said with the serene air of one
who had reason to suspect, were all places as
faultlessly filled, this world would be a very
different caravansary. "Come, child, let us
move on."

Thus Vroni, from one point of vision and
another, got dissolving views of what Gireaud
called *le beau monde's* curious antics, — of
what the higher, so-called educated classes
who needed not to toil or spin deemed expe-
dient and indispensable, in short, of their
standard of greatness; and pondered somewhat, but not unhealthily much, upon these
things. The routine appointed for her by
her master held her in firm discipline, his
ample ægis never failed; through the more or
less perilous flunkydom of the great house —
the snobbish valets were at first fresh country
lads who but imitated their master's pretty
manners — the girl passed unmolested. She
had scarcely an adventure.

Once a piano-man, as she dubbed him, a
well dressed, smart sort of person with a
waxed moustache, who had superintended the

transport of a grand piano from town and, after setting it on its legs, tried it at some length with musical touch and haunting melodies, found her leaning by the door just in his path — her head thrown back, her brown eyes dreamy.

In the gloating sultan humor of his kind he pinched her cheek and stooped suggestively.

" *Wait!* " was the fierce response, and Vroni " up and at " him with a resounding whack on his right ear.

" *Donnerwetter!* " muttered the man, but laughed and turned to look as she fled down the corridor. Her anger spent, she gave the trifling episode no thought.

On some sudden quest for the lord of the larder whose exalted need, rejecting new-laid eggs, sweet cream, fat capons, savory herbs, demanded things still fresher, sweeter, richer, fatter, more aromatic, rare, and marvellous, choicer than earth's choicest — say a roc's egg, or *la rose trois fois exquise*, she for a brief season passed frequently a quiet figure sitting alone in a corner of the courtyard, a man in uniform, evidently an officer's *Bursch*, and stared well at him because of his hair, which was lint white and standing up thick like a brush.

One day he was holding a big spaniel's nose between his knees. She, a little blue jug in her hand, stopped and watched him solicitously extract a thorn from the animal's head.

"Did you get it all?" she demanded eagerly, drawing near.

He looked up and nodded, but instantly dropped his eyes, abashed by the nearness of the beatific vision he had for days watched flitting hither and thither, patted the dog awkwardly, and let him go.

"What's your name?" she asked, not ungraciously for her.

The big fellow again raised a pair of honest childlike eyes of bluest blue, and stared helplessly at her.

"Well?" she said curtly. "Don't you know your own name?"

His mouth twitched nervously, but no word issued from it in the radiant presence of Our Lady of the Jug.

"Towhead, I doubt not," she suggested, her smile mocking, her manner hard.

Then the dumb spake.

"Towhead they've called me all my life," he answered gently, with thick, slow utterance, but not without manliness. "My name is Tiber. I'm Count Benno's extra man."

Before the steady blue of his eyes, and a certain patience in his voice, her mood wavered.

"*Ach, so 'was!*" she murmured, frowned, turned brusquely on her heel and walked off.

The man sighed from the very depths of his long riding boots, into which his body seemed to sink disconsolate.

But presently he started and sat up alert, for she came tripping down from the house, her white apron greeting him like a flag of truce, her beautiful hair shining in the sun, on her lips glad tidings, and in her hands a heaped-up plate and a foaming tankard.

"Towhead," she began, "'t is no harm thou art slow of tongue. 'T were better others jabbered less. Take it not ill that I was hasty, Towhead. 'T is, 't is," she hesitated, "'t is my way ofttimes," smiling negligently with a sort of imperial candor. "Here's some fine bits I have begged for thee from M'sieu Armand. Art a brave lad and good to dogs," she concluded, artlessly patronizing, as if he himself were some big four-footed thing she was patting on the back. "So there! And now, good-day."

Poor Tiber saw her go, and other days he saw her pass, but always far away. Never again at Schloss Waldmohr did our Sunny Lady of the Jug descend upon his humble awkwardness, to make his heart beat high, his tongue cleave to the roof of his mouth, and his whole being bask in inexplicably miserable blessedness or thrice-blessed misery. Once on the high-road she smiled and nodded brightly, as he was exercising Count Benno's Fuchs; again by the river she remembered him, and was not too proud to give him friendly greeting, though both times she was walking with a most distinguished-looking gentleman in a top hat. But Tiber got no ghost of a chance to speak to her. For it happened that during the remaining fortnight of Count Benno's stay, Maître Giraud, Chef de Cuisine and Cordon Bleu, required of his willing and fleet-footed messenger nothing whatever that necessitated voyages in the vicinity of the courtyard. His prolific imaginings, one and all, floated persistently in a contrary direction.

When, after a twelve months' absence, Vroni shone again upon Hexenfels — the count and countess having closed the house to spend a winter in Egypt — she was approximately a trained French cook, had somewhat softened manners, and called her headache her *migraine*, but otherwise, as Dionysius the weaver perceived with his first searching look in her glad good eyes, was the self-same Mädel, and he thanked his God for her as they walked hand-in-hand through their meagre grain-fields.

It was again the time of the mighty north winds, swinging east and back again, swift as a cruel thought, — uprooting stout trees, and uplifting roofs, for all their freight of stones. Vroni would whisk together the ingredients of an aërial, foam-born omelette with a virtuosity which left her mother struggling between open-mouthed admiration and stubborn prejudice in favor of ancestral methods, and a "pan-cake with a bite to it." But in that frugal household was small demand for the girl's unsuspected adeptship. The long winter was staring them in the face, and the great snowdrifts which settled early, and lay so long on the Rough Alp, would soon be closing round them.

Dionysius longed to keep her always near him, so fond, so clinging, so sad with pre-

science was his tenderness for his child. But
Agathe argued to what end? and counted
often, and with cheerful clinking, the last
little pile of gold, earned at Schloss Waldmohr. The maid had begun briskly; 't were
folly, sin, and shame to stop her now. When
he was a bit ailing, he always hung his head;
but, *Du lieber Gott*, was that a reason why she
should sit idle all winter, and hold his hand,
for all the world as if they were courting?

By the time Hexenfels lay snowbound, all
laughter and sunshine had fled from the
lonely cottage under the crag. Agathe, self-
sufficient, bustled, toiled, and talked; while
Dionysius, sallower, aging visibly, silent,
languid, worked when he had strength enough,
— and when, indeed, he had not — and pined
in secret for his heart's dearest, his youngest,
his nestling, who this time had spread her
wings for a longer, stronger flight.

V

"ARE you sure you can do all this?" demanded the Countess von Vallade, examining, with surprise, a copious document signed with the simplicity of greatness, *Gireaud, Schloss Waldmohr* —and glancing alternately at its explicit statements, and their youthful subject.

"If he says so," replied Vroni, who had spelled out as yet but a mere fraction of the long and eloquent tribute to her skill, which he, with tears in his eyes, had implored her to regard all her life as her most precious possession and talisman.

"While you have that you will never want. To-day you snap your fingers. One day you will comprehend, my poor child. See, I give it you in this strong leather case, with a stout lock and key. Keep your receipt book also in it. Guard both as your life. It is my solemn parting word, my little friend, — my

dawning colleague, I hesitate not to pronounce you, I, Gireaud."

The good soul also presented her with a
beautiful framed photograph of the castle.
Across the whole lower margin of the picture was writ large: *Residence of Armand
Gireaud* from May 3, 189– to Sept. 2, 189–,
sixteen months and seventeen days.

> *"Nur die Lumpen sind bescheiden ;*
> *Brave freuen sich der That."*

The countess was seated at her writing-
table, — one of those dwarfed and painful little
monsters called specifically ladies' writing-
tables, ornate, unsteady, and bow-legged; its
small surface so littered with cheap bronzes,
statuettes, crystal toys, vases, and other fragile nonsense, no robust thought had room
to stretch itself. One would never have
suspected the modern meretricious thing possessed a secret drawer. Putting up her lorgnette she dubiously surveyed the young girl
standing before her.

"She is incredibly young to be able to do
entire dinners," remarked the lady in French,
to her charming daughter, who, reclining in
a low chair, was doing nothing at all, unless

candidly admiring one's shoes may be called
an occupation.

"Clotilde gave us heavenly dinners at
Waldmohr — simply heavenly!" returned the
fair Nelka, with a dreamy smile that would
have inspired a poet.

"Exactly, and this man actually asserts
this girl did a good part of them."

"Try her — she looks so nice," said Jella,
amiably.

"Her appearance is against her. She is
too pretty for her station."

"I like them pretty. If I could have my
way, all the frights should be suppressed by
royal decree," Nelka retorted, pretty enough
herself to dare to be magnanimous.

"Yes, yes; but beauty in one's kitchen is
startlingly out of place."

"It does not hurt the cooking!" suggested
Vroni, grave and impartial.

Nelka laughed aloud.

"You understand French?"

"Oh, as much as that."

Again Nelka laughed, Vroni knew not why.

"Any more?" asked the young lady,
amused.

Now Vroni, the unsubdued, was beginning

to feel strangely ill at ease under the discomfort of an ordeal at best confusing and disheartening — as even ladies of quality might perceive, should superior beings stand them up, subject them to cold and vaguely inimical scrutiny, and cross-examine them solely as to what they were good for; but she answered sturdily: —

"Not the fancy words my master sometimes spoke; but useful talk he taught me: the names of kitchen things and cookery — and *mille tonnerres* and *saprelotte* and such," she added, unsmiling and literal.

"Well, she is a character," began the countess in English. "I hope she is not always so familiar."

"It's not her fault. I led her on. Besides, where's the harm?"

"You seem to have several names on your certificate. What are you usually called?"

"Vroni Lindl is my name."

"Well, Vroni," interrogated the countess, her voice both haughty and suspicious, — that chilly, remote, pre-judging voice with which women, otherwise not ungentle, elect to open relationships with their humble handmaids, — "are you sure you are quite steady? No followers, eh? Because nothing of the sort could be thought of an instant in a house of this character."

Vroni, greatly enjoying neither lorgnette nor voice, and finding the question altogether preposterous, flushed and frowned, but, meeting the kind bright gaze of the young comtesse, recovered herself, and smiling shrewdly in reminiscence of floating red cravat-ends, and blushing swains enthroned on stiles, said, with enchanting carelessness, looking straight at Nelka: —

"Oh — they!"

Instructions as to privileges, perquisites, and other details followed, and were quickly settled. It was evident Vroni was most eager to come, and not greedy of gain. But imperceptible to them, to herself undefinable, was the sudden depression in her heart's barometer which indicated many degrees less sunshine than when she crossed the threshold of that cheerful morning-room. Gireaud, though masterful, had from the first consulted her, asked her what she thought and liked, led her to tell him of her home and people, and otherwise paid tacit respect to her personality, to that unruly little personality which, whether reprimanded or adored, had never in its rude home known neglect. But the Count-ess von Vallade, pre-assuming this beautiful and fresh young thing was but a contingent section of the household machinery, — a vexa-tious section indeed, apt to generate excess of friction, and require frequent renewal, — showed no human interest, spoke no human word. And Vroni resented this deeply if dumbly. Not even the good and gay face of the Comtesse Nelka offered compensation for the unmerited, and as yet uncomprehended affront.

"Now, Vroni," said the finely scathing voice, "do you suppose you are old enough to get on well with the other servants? Some of them have their peculiarities, no doubt."

"That's all right. I have mine."

"I must explain," the voice continued, but paused, while quite a different one, though from the same larynx, uttered a smooth aside in English: "Nelka dear, I really wish you'd not encourage her so. Your too obvious de-light in her pertness only makes her worse. She has no idea of manners; but happily one never sees her kind after the first."

"I think her manners lovely — quite too lovely."

"Vroni, I warn you, I never listen to complaints. Whoever complains goes. It is a rule of the house. There are five servants beside yourself and the coachman. They are rather old, and set in their ways; but they have been with me long. The change is always with the cook. Somehow, of late I cannot keep one. I suppose it is some *chicane*, but I never interfere. Of course it is your duty to conciliate. You really are so young," — at this heavy charge the voice augmented its asperity, — "so unusually young, for so responsible a position, I think it looks altogether very unpromising, in spite of your references from Waldmohr. They are excellent, I do not deny. But, after all, one never knows."

During this harangue, Vroni wisely kept her eyes on the comtesse, and thereby revived a fair amount of native spirit.

"I 'm quick," the girl replied, in her candid way, addressing exclusively the one she liked; "but I 'm pretty good-hearted. My bark is worse than my bite. They need not be afraid of me, no, not a bit, only — " straightening herself, in unconscious imitation of her illustrious chief, and like him looking about an instant, with battle-light in her eye — "I stand no nonsense when I 'm doing a dinner." Descending to ordinary human levels, she said reflectively: "Five? There were nineteen at the castle, beside strangers. Oh, yes, I can tackle five of them!" nodding with easy confidence at Nelka.

"Take her instantly, mamma, she 's delicious, and let her make a lovely *bisque* this very night. It 's Eck's favorite soup."

"Where he is going, he 'll get no *bisques*."

"All the more reason to please him now, besides — "

"Well?"

Nelka colored.

"Nothing. I 've forgotten. I mean you would not like it. But — " she hesitated.

"Little chatterer!" said the mother, with an indulgence that blandly waived Eck Flemming, as subject of serious discussion, completely out of court. Turning to Vroni, she asked languidly: —

"How did you happen to come to me, my good girl? Who sent you just at a kitchen-crisis?"

"I sent myself," quoth Vroni, with bright emphasis, "to the gracious Comtesse Nelka. I made up my mind long ago, I wanted to work for her. It was the first time I saw her. She wore a pink frock, and they would not let her jump a wee little hedge. So I came straight here."

"I thank you, Vroni," returned the young lady, warmly. "I remember — and it is sweet of you."

"And if there 'd been no place for me, I would have waited," the girl said, speaking soft like her father, and looking at Nelka in a way that touched her, it was so full of frank and glad devotion. "It was the Comtesse Nelka I wanted, and nobody else. Somehow I had to come here."

When, an hour later, Vroni reported that she was engaged at the Vallade's, Melchior's elderly wife exclaimed grudgingly:—

"Some do have the devil's own luck! Good, steady, sober, experienced women, out of employment on all sides; and little whipper-snappers bounce down from the hill-country, as bold as ye please, and wheedle themselves into notice with their pert tongues."

"'T was their own tongues that wagged," stated Vroni, placid, and historically accurate. "*Kauderwelsch* mostly."

"It is a fine house," declared Melchior, with unction. "Their coachman belongs to my club — a most respectable man. They are much esteemed at Court. Must be prudent, Vroni, and smooth-spoken."

"Every bird chirps according to his beak. Besides it's not my talk they hire."

"I should like to know what they do hire!" said Jakobine, sourly.

"But Vroni has good references," hazarded Melchior; "conduct signed by the Countess Waldmohr."

"It's a good deal she knows of my conduct," Vroni remarked cheerfully. "She hardly saw me. If she signed, 't was the housekeeper told her to."

Melchior looked slightly pained by the indecorum of this suggestion, but, ignoring it, continued: —

"Then the long French one that nobody can read. It makes a fine appearance."

"Appearance!" sniffed Jakobine.

"Of course they don't really amount to much," he hastened to concede.

"No, they don't!" Vroni asserted brightly. "Just what I say. Bits of paper. Who cares for them? Still the lady read the French one, and screwed up her face, and looked at me for all the world like old Blasius buying a cow."

"Vroni!" groaned her brother. "Dost think that is the way to find favor with the great?"

"Hast no modesty at all and no fear?" demanded Jakobine.

"Fear?" Vroni repeated, staring with raised eyebrows.

"Yes, fear," rejoined the woman, impatiently. "Of not suiting, of not doing things right, of not knowing how to behave, since thou hast precious little experience, and less sense."

"Truly, I had not thought of that," said the young girl, slowly. "Besides," she added, after a moment, joyfully, "seest, Jakobine, I know a lot."

"Self-praise goes but little way, eh, Melchior?"

"'T is as thou sayest," said the man, but coughed behind his hand in deprecation, for somehow he felt a sneaking delight in the coming of his sister; — besides her prospects looked promising.

Jakobine drove him with tighter curb than

he the king's grays. Ten years his senior, and of forbidding countenance, she was a paragon of respectability, which he very properly deemed more precious than comeliness. By wedding the daughter of a head-coachman, prudent Melchior had secured rapid advancement in his chosen career. He had married, as the saying is, straight into the business. It was not his fault that the man inopportunely died, and another had succeeded with his own progeny to consider.

No, Melchior had made no error in his calculations. They were based indeed upon the obvious tactics of the great and wise, the world's noblest families, princes of the blood, potentates, sovereigns by the grace of God. Jakobine had brought to her marriage a modest dowry, considerable worldly ambition, shrewdness in practical matters, thrift, diligence, and inflexible devotion to the observances of the Church. Even Sister Corona and Sebastian had strongly commended his choice. He had gained precisely what he sought, and what he prized highest; yet, though he dared not admit it plainly, — even to himself alone in the dark, — he was hopelessly puzzled to discover that a human lot, exhaling the quintessence of respectability, could sit so ghastly heavy on a man. Sometimes he longed for the Rough Alp. Often he sadly wished he had a child, but took care not to say it. Unloving, not even kind, Jakobine owned obtrusively, as property, the man whom the Holy Church had given her, and was morbidly jealous of every woman who passed him, unseeing, in the streets. He squirmed well to keep the peace. His only joys, though alloyed with deep grievances, he found in the daily pomps of his vocation. Herein, too, he resembled not a little his exalted prototypes.

Into this fatiguing interior had suddenly burst Vroni's nonchalant beauty, her audacious charm, her rather insolent good luck. Jakobine, from the moment they met, could but regard her with sullen resentment. It was only yesterday she had come. Already the older woman's grudge was deep-rooted as a family feud.

"Ye look little enough like brother and sister," she now remarked, with singular acerbity. "'T will not be believed. 'T will make talk."

The two, never having considered this phenomenon, began to scrutinize each other attentively, perhaps for the first time in their lives. Nothing could be truer than Jakobine's reproach.

"Being but halves," suggested Vroni, studying Melchior's smooth-shaved, sandy, and freckled visage. His eyes were light and far-sighted, his expression sanctimonious. Consciousness of close connection with Throne and State, together with Jakobine's unwearying whip, and his tendency to enjoy the gloomy side of religion, had dropped the corners of his mouth in sharp furrows.

Vroni mustered him critically.

"Hast a big bare mouth, Melchior. Art strange to me so, and a good bit uglier. Didst use to deck thy upper lip with flax."

The elder brother, not ill-pleased to assume a superior and didactic tone toward one who had hitherto treated him with small respect, replied solemnly: —

"No bearded man would be employed in any fine house, Vroni, — let alone the palace."

"'T is only country wenches that know not that," said Jakobine.

"Men may not wear their own hair as they like?"

"'T is not genteel."

"*Ätschgäbele!*" cried Vroni — an altogether untranslatable expression, — common, innocent, juvenile, and conveying frank derision, which was precisely what she felt. Again she inspected him.

"Yet at Hexenfels didst laugh, and many a time," she said, in answer to her own cogitations.

"Hast grown a tall and tidy maid," he rejoined kindly, for her brilliant brownness pleased him well, in spite of himself, and though he knew it to be but dross.

"Nice modest girls without looks get on better in the town," warned Jakobine, grimly.

"Thou, Melchior, were I a man, and did I drive four splendid horses stepping proudly — "

"I can drive six — eight — more — as many as any man," he broke in, one quick and youthful gleam of honest pride lighting his staid features.

"Surely!" she cried, nodding in delighted sympathy. "Well, then, I 'd hold my head up high as a king, seest, Melchior, and I 'd crack my whip at all creation, and I 'd laugh and sing, and blow my horn, and come sweeping through green woods, the sunshine on my

cheek; and when I sat down to stretch my
long boots and take my beer, half-a-dozen
tidy maids should run to wait on me, and I 'd
have a merry word for each and all.   That 's
what I 'd do, Melchior!"

With a gasp of pious consternation, he
turned to his wife.

"She means a — *postillion!*" ejaculated the
shocked king's coachman.

"I mean a whole man," said Vroni, merrily.
"I spied him when I went to the Fair."

"Hast spied many such, I make no doubt,"
flung in Jakobine, inexplicably incensed and
with fathomless suspicion.

"*Na* — that thou knowst no difference
'twixt high and low!" exclaimed Melchior,
aghast before so deplorable ignorance.   "Why,
if any of *us* acted that disgraceful, or half so
common-like, and let-out in our manners, we 'd
lose our position without warning, and serve
us right.   'T is not easy to keep it at best,"
he continued, diverging into gloom; "what
with the rivalry and favoritism, and the pressure from above, and the pushing from below.
For some of those new chaps are starting
up like mushrooms, and Heaven alone knows
where they 'll stop, and whom they 'll oust, —

the head-coachman being a most uncertain man, — times having changed for the worse, Jakobine." She acknowledged with a series of austerely recapitulating nods this pious tribute to her father's shade.

"Yes, 't is even so, *so ist's*. But thou, Vroni, knowst naught of Court life."

"Nay, nor would I, if it taketh the marrow out of a man, and setteth him a-whining."

"Seest, Vroni, at Court there be underground ways to all things. Steady must a man go, as on the tight-rope. Wise as the serpent, harmless as the dove. Careful to offend no soul; friendly with all, trusting none, and to the great, most humble."

"Ha, it must suit thee well!" she said dryly; "couldst ever nimbly duck to right or left."

"Truly, 't would wonder thee much, Vroni, didst know what I know," he insisted sepulchrally.

She looked at him with a shrewd and faintly ironical smile.

"*Ei, ei*, Melchior, art grown so wise?"

"Hast no notion of our instructions," he went on with mournful complacency, "of the loads we must remember! 'T is a sore burden

to the mind.   Seest, Vroni, wouldst never of
thyself think it.   'T is they that look most
English, get promoted fastest.   'T is the Ber-
lin way.   His Majesty is most particular.
But the Queen, — *O Weh!* I had the honor to
drive her Majesty out yesterday.   Time was,
I did drive the royalties out every day, but of
late I be so much neglected, I fear my grays
will take on flesh, howe'er I keep them gently
moving by myself.   A great thing, Vroni, to
drive her Majesty, but 't is awful on the
nerves.   Not for thy life must thou sneeze;
and if a fly tickles thy nose, thou must needs
let him tickle as though thou wert a man of
wood not flesh.   The word 's gone forth: English, every inch — though the sky falls."

"English?   How English?   What 's English?"

Puffing with vanity beneath his lamenta-
tions, Melchior suddenly accentuated himself — intensified beyond belief his habitual
demeanor.

Incredibly solemn, rigid, impassable, ex-
pressionless, a human automaton, he sat
straight as a rod, his wrists in position, and
gazed, as it were, between his leader's ears.

"O Melchior, O Melchior, dost call it

English?" laughed Vroni, in wild mirth. "Truly, 't is like a sheep. Wast ever somewhat like a sheep, seest, Melchior! So now canst make a rare good mutton-head to please the king."

"It is the way approved at Court," he rejoined, severely.

Standing before him in the well-scoured place of torment he called his home, the young girl regarded him long, her merriment gradually merging into grave inquiry, her carelessness followed by coolly intelligent reflection. It was her first day in a large town. A whirl of novel scenes had opened before her rustic mind, a multitude of vaguely unappetizing impressions had been roused no less by the lady of high and mighty degree than by the cringing charioteer, and Jakobine's presence was distinctly grisly. Far off, in clear contrast, she beheld a simple figure, and her thoughtful gaze still on her brother, she said gently: —

"Of all ways, the way that in all things pleases me — 't is my father's way."

VI

VRONI had run bareheaded in summer sun
and winter blasts. This was the fashion in
Hexenfels. There, girls never wore hats, —
even to church, — thereby saving much expense, perplexity of choice, and the chagrin
of finding one's apex overtopped by one's
neighbor's. So far as can be ascertained,
these hatless maids rejoiced in an immunity
from colds unknown to those protected from
the inclemency of the weather by the most
fashionable bonnets. Now a bit of white
cap perched on her shining braids compactly
reefed; she wore a very long and resplendent
white apron; and every other morning, when
she went to market carried a big brown basket
on her arm.

She walked well, far better, for instance, than
Nelka von Vallade, who lacked the advantages
of Vroni's early training in carrying heavy things
on the head up and down goat paths. Erect,
free, unconcerned, she passed swiftly through

busy streets where people turned to look at her, she was so fresh and charming a picture. They too thought her — whatever their urban rendition of the rustic phrase — a tidy maid. But not her rich coloring, not her lithe and spirited step, transformed careless glances into surprised scrutiny so much as her atmosphere, — a certain radiant audacity of health and gladness, and her young smile as she walked among strangers, — a vague, sweet, fearless smile, which her heart flung abroad in blithe greeting to the whole great world.

No wonder she smiled. She was consciously rejoicing in her strength and freedom. She had never imagined anything so entertaining as town life. In Hexenfels, one week was like another; Waldmohr was pleasant and lively, but she was serving a close apprenticeship; here each day, each hour, brought fresh delights. Moreover, till now, she had been under nominal tutelage. Her mother's habitual chiding, her father's anxious watchfulness, and at the castle Armand Gircaud's puissant guardianship had never failed. Now she was her own mistress, and gloried in it. Every restraining voice had ceased. Melchior,

it is true, and more especially Jakobine, at the
mere sight of the girl's buoyancy, were prone
to strike Cassandra-notes; but she saw her
brother far less frequently than Dionysius
the weaver fondly imagined in his wistful
pictures of her. On her fortnightly free
Sunday she joined them for their walk and
glass of beer in some wayside inn, and
hardly heeded that Jakobine was repellent
and Melchior henpecked, so enchanting were
the songs, the laughter, and the friendliness
of happy faces.

Vroni in her plebeian circles could not help
now and then hearing comments upon her
beauty. No more could Nelka von Vallade
upon hers in the best society. Vroni was
beginning to comprehend that she was personally pleasing. Nelka, in her own case, had
been aware of a similarly palatable truth all
her life — yet bore herself with a frank and
simple spirit. Vroni too passed among
men's blatantly admiring stares, — for which
Jakobine sternly reprimanded her, instead
of them, — and was, a little, indeed, but not
much, less unconscious than when she used
to run wild in the mountains — immuring old
shrews and setting walnut-trees ablaze. In her

heart dwelt as yet no thought that could sorely grieve her angel, or Dionysius the weaver, — their standard for her being perhaps pretty much the same thing.

Father and daughter, loving each other ardently, wrote inarticulate little letters, as was the fashion in Hexenfels. They always took their pens in hand to pen a few lines to say they were in good health and hoped the other was the same, after which, with fresh impetus, they stated succinctly that they, *Gottlob!* enjoyed up to date very good health. Dionysius then penned his duty to her gracious master and mistress, and commended himself to them, —under the innocent impression that they must occasionally condescend to some sort of human intercourse with his dear child,— and he hoped they and all their gracious family were enjoying very good health. Further, he hoped Melchior and his dear Frau Jakobine were enjoying very good health. Vroni, in her turn, expressed equally explicit solicitude as to each and all of her relatives in the village. They began rather low down on a small sheet of paper with lines well apart, and by the time they had penned all their obligatory hygienic preliminaries, their fingers felt cramped from the unwonted exercise, their brains dull, and never by any accident did they say what they really meant. That letters eventually might serve as means toward this end, they seemed not to suspect.

Coptic cannot better screen secrets than did their bald missives. Agathe's indeed were in a certain sense a success, for she wrote simply and solely to chronicle felicitous domestic events among her four-footed friends, and achieved what she undertook. But Vroni, living in what seemed to her one endless round of delight, wishing always he were near to share her joy, loving him truly, though so glad at heart, said naught of all this, and remarked staidly every week, " Town pleases me fairly well," — the set phrase being what she had learned to pen. Dionysius, wasting away physically, eating his heart out with longing and brooding tenderness, transmuting his failing life-forces into one incessant benediction, never varied his academic treatise upon everybody's physical condition. His great love and pain were dumb, except for three poor words that crept in after the penning was all done, and huddled themselves shyly in some corner: *Sei brav*, *Mädel*, and that homely, " Be good, little girl," had for her small significance, at least no thrilling undertone.

It was doubtless presumptuous for a person in Vroni's station to be so inordinately happy. She was by far the happiest creature in the Vallade house, possibly in the whole town. She thoroughly liked her work, and the new sense of power it gave her. In every respect she proceeded with marvellous fidelity upon Armand Gireaud's lines, was a credit to his methods and his perspicuity, and brought to her daily tasks sufficient temperament and vitality to equip half-a-dozen average women. She was exceedingly busy, but she had never been anything else. Her *Herrschaft* made large demands upon her resources, it being the dinner-season; she was equal to them; she met them with the composure of an old campaigner. She possessed indeed a secret source of strength, her book, annotated and filled out by the Master's hand.

She was continually discovering new charges, warnings, appeals, and hints, as if he had foreseen every imaginable predicament. Then the innumerable *menus* he had " composed " for her. Lunch for ten ladies — young. Ditto for ditto, — mature. (Gireaud had to be very angry be-

fore he would perceive that women could grow
old.)   Dinners of all sizes and *nuances*, poetic,
æsthetic, aldermanic, for the clergy, the *haute
finance*, the army, artists, statesmen, royalties,
and every sort of mixed company conceivable
in polite circles.

Once Count Benno sent out from the dining-
room to know if she could get him up a game
supper for eight men, cold but *"pyramidal"*
good, — the adjectives refer to the supper, by
no means to the men, — and have it at his
rooms in a garrison town near by, by eleven
o'clock on the following night.   She said she
could.   Her chef had instructed her always to
say she could, whatever was required.   That
night she was considering the special nature of
Count Benno's demand, and turned the pages of
her book, thinking to make some careful com-
bination; when, suddenly, she came upon the
very thing she wanted: " Choice Late Supper
for Young Men — *Lively*."   It was there —
even to the wines.   It seemed like magic.
Count Benno said the feast was *" colossal."*

Vroni promptly proved a match for her
elderly colleagues, and imbued them with the
healthful notion that she would do them no
harm, provided they would behave themselves.

Her views succeeded by force of their originality, their singleness of aim, and her peculiarly lucid mode of exposition. Hitherto, a solid phalanx had routed every cook. This cook routed the phalanx. Former cooks had sought to ingratiate themselves with the august body, failed, lost their tempers under impossible demands and incessant badgering, complained, appealed to supreme authority; hence moved on.

It was a merry little game. The butler and the Swiss maid had a stiff bet on Vroni's exit. With the youthful rustic, the worthies thought to have easy scoring. She, little used to impudence — except her own — and not at all to petty tyranny, stared at them in surprise the first day, on the second frowned and watched them warily, and on the third, without subtlety or exhortation, without suspecting that she was an able tactician, simply starved out the garrison. Having provided nothing for the servants' table, she locked her larder, put her keys in her pocket, and went to bed. It was a song without words. Were there curses in response, she heard them not.

On the following day, they, one and all, wished her a civil good-morning and eyed her

furtively to discover her mood. She revealed
it uncompromisingly. Turning toward them,
her arms akimbo, — visibly possessing her
domain and measuring them with dauntless
eyes, — she spoke ruggedly, like Agathe, and
though tolerably used now to the more formal
"you," relapsed, as always in vital moments,
into her familiar dialect: —

"Ye townfolk! Ha! Where I stand 't is
my kitchen! Mark ye this. 'T is once for all
I speak. *Saprelotte!*"

Whereupon she gave them an excellent
breakfast. They found her a generous and
gallant conqueror, and as they knew her
better, most benevolent for her years; always
ready to take trouble to gratify any little taste
of 'theirs, not merely in her special province,
but willing to do a good bit of sewing for one,
an errand on her way from market, or any
service in her power; even capable of a volun-
tary and cordial relinquishment of her precious
Sunday outing in favor of a maid with an ill
mother, or a sweetheart sailing, or some other
real or alleged cause for irregular absence.
But they discovered also that Vroni was two
distinct personalities: as young girl, sunny,
kindly, if rough and ready of tongue, hot,

but sweet-tempered, — for tempers may be that, as well as cold and sour, — easy, unexacting, in short what they called a good fellow; but as head of her department most inexorably masterful.

She seemed to have framed for her private guidance a species of Code Napoleon, or, since unwritten, Brehon Laws, perhaps, which she never discussed. But they learned to comprehend. For the instant one of them transgressed the smallest of her unannounced but inflexible precepts, by a hair's-breadth, infringed upon what she, from a professional point of view, regarded as her liberty of action, — her official dignity, — or offended her sense of justice, the entire group was condemned to suffer the pangs of hunger, — the innocent with the guilty. Each, therefore, was incited to do constable service, and keep his neighbor in order, those with the heartiest appetites working most strenuously; and peace reigned as never before within those precincts. Vroni neither pondered her course nor recalled it with elation. She simply and instinctively promoted the survival of the fittest — herself. Her procedure was probably but a reflex action of which the motor should be sought in

ancient days, when Agathe implanted in her
little erring daughter's mind the imperative
association between naughtiness and a yearning stomach.

Vroni had, in her own sphere, business
enough richly to sustain her own inquiry;
moreover, curiosity as to the affairs of others
lay not in her disposition. But the myriad
facts, fables, and inferences incessantly filter-
ing down from high sources through the serving substratum reached her consciousness and
were passively absorbed. Old family servants
command their own sort of Röntgen-ray. Pitifully bare and quivering the Vallade family
heart lay before the trained stolidity of those
grave men in livery, mute and decorous as the
tall carved chair-backs behind which they
effaced themselves, the massive sideboard about
which they noiselessly hovered; and the deft
still maid, brushing her lady's hair night after
night, read as an open book the tired worldly
thoughts revolving in their vicious circle.

With some yet not over-abundant malice,
with benevolence varying according to purely
subjective conditions, certainly with not a whit
less charity than my lady herself employed in
doing what she euphemistically called "talk-

ing over" her friends, the employed, *en petit comité*, minutely and often discussed their employers, their foibles and idiosyncrasies, their aims, struggles, and chagrins, and, with unflinching correctness, their inadequate budget. Thus higher education reached Vroni by her ears.

Her eyes, too, were not idle. In her pleasant and commodious realm, she was stationed as it were between two worlds, and serenely aloof from both. On the one side, she looked over a spacious garden slope upon the backs of towering buildings in a busy street. Across the space, between two houses, men and women of the work-a-day world tramped with their burdens. Nearest her was a piano manufactory. Through many tiers of windows men were visible at benches and tables, — men seated, standing, moving, shaping, fashioning, hammering. It seemed good, clean work, and cheerful. Beyond was a tricot factory, a dingy place. At certain hours a file of rough women streamed in and out. She could perceive their crowded rows of heads in their treadmill. It looked to her like a prison, — and stuffy, coughy work she was sure.

In that street, early on rainy mornings, hum-

ble women passed, overladen, — a basket on
the head, heavy parcels under the arms, and
sometimes struggling also with a dislocated
umbrella, — while long wet calico skirts wob-
bled about their ankles and solicited rheuma-
tism; men similarly weighted strode by with
comparative ease. In Vroni's church, of which
she could see the spire, they told her every
back was fitted to its burden. Truly the trousers might be, likewise, she reflected. "It were
no sin, for Comtesse Nelka wears such on her
wheel. But did a poor woman dare — *na, na !*"

But to such things she gave but a quick
careless glance when her duties happened to
call her in that direction to set something away
to cool in the store-room, or sunning on the
kitchen veranda. The veranda suited her
vastly, for it was high and looked toward distant hills and free skies. She pranced out for
an instant often. Sometimes she spied other
white-capped cooks on their verandas, and
smiled with gratified ambition because none
was so young as she, then smiled again in a
better way, with a good thought of Gir[e]aud.
Many of these impressions were as swift and
light as her whisking of eggs. She had in
truth more important business than to stare at

her neighbors or waste much thought upon
them.

Far up the work-a-day street, where it wound
toward suburbs out of sight was a common
from whence the monotonous strains of a
carrousel sometimes proceeded. She had seen
the thing on a Sunday, its painted cars with
horses' heads always going round and round
and never arriving. There stood too a great
building used for circuses and various sorts
of meetings. Late at night, long after she was
in bed, she had once in the still air heard the
dull irregular patter of many feet approaching
along the lower road and a group of men and
women marching and singing vehemently. By
the time they reached the piano manufactory
she could distinguish the words of the oft-re-
peated refrain : —

> " It grows and blooms for human bliss,
>   The Red Republic ! "

but what manner of thing that was she had
no notion, or why after human bliss the song
came to a violent end with a sound of scuffling,
hoarse altercation, and a couple of shrill in-
sistent whistles. Her day's work was done,
her market book in order, her conscience

tranquil, so she turned over and fell sound asleep.

In the opposite direction was what she called the play-day world.

Now that the great trees which should discreetly veil her domain were leafless, she could see across the court a short section of the aristocratic street, unmolested by traffic, unsullied by the passage of heavy vans, trucks, or any vehicle remotely suggestive of sweat of brows, horny hands of toil, or anything trite and repugnant. Smart carriages were continually dashing across this field of vision. So many, many carriages, shining like her copper saucepans and silver platters, going on and on like the *carrousel*-carts, and seeming never to arrive, for she could not see them turn into the little drive that led to the Vallade portals or stop at other doors.

Ladies and gentlemen, but mostly ladies, hour after hour, day after day, week after week, year after year, paying calls, and always so awfully glad to see one another. *Sapristi!* Always two men on the box, dark green men or brown or blue or whitish, mostly young and foolish-looking, quite like Hans, Seppl, and Michel — and always one high on a cushion, terribly English, like Melchior, and the other with folded arms and his nose in the air, as if he had finished all his work for one life at least.

Occasionally Melchior himself drove past, exercising the royal grays. The servants always ran to tell her he was coming, that she might station herself in time. They felt huge exaltation in gazing at the cushions upon which a monarch sometimes sat, were flattered by the subtle approach of that sacred upholstery to themselves through Vroni and her eminent brother, and always expected her to evince some reasonable pride in him. But she was an odd stick. If engaged in intricate work which she thought ought not to be dropped, hardly thanking them for their rush and flurry, she flatly refused to stir, "Not for a regiment of king's horses and brothers to boot," and "that haughty" was instantly telegraphed through the mansion. When, however, she deemed it compatible with higher schemes, she deigned to occupy a pantry window of observation and await the pageant.

Conscious of rectitude and many eyes upon him, Melchior always came on slowly and held himself superb as a candlestick. As he passed the pantry, he permitted the merest ghost of a grin to distort one side of his face, which lent him a somewhat paralytic charm. Although Vroni laughed, and frowned, and muttered disdainfully: *Ach, was! Englisch!* and gave the plump chicken or whatever she had on hand a good slap, she rather liked to look across the court and see him majestically traverse that short section of road. English or no English, he was her brother and a bit of home. As for Melchior, it became one of the few joys of his impeccable but sombre existence; and as he took care not to mention it to Jakobine, it possessed for him an almost clandestine fascination.

But the magnet that drew Vroni quickest to some convenient observatory was Comtesse Nelka, in whatever garb that winning damsel sallied forth, and whether driving or on foot, whether indeed all that Vroni could discern of her were her carriage lights as she whirled off to a dinner or ball. She, too, was always like the *carrousel*, going and going, paying calls incessantly, breathlessly busy and nearly always out in the evenings.

Vroni eagerly caught even the most fleeting and remote glimpse of the radiant creature whom face to face she rarely saw. But the little comtesse always stopped and had a good word to say wherever they might meet, were it in the street and Vroni with her market basket. Whatever was of consummate excellence and delicacy in Vroni's achievements, she secretly dedicated to Comtesse Nelka, and with a sort of happy boyishness — like the allegiance of some stanch little page for his sovereign lady — served her ever zealously, not repining that her gracious presence was so rare a boon, — content in perfect service.

VII

THE debate had been long, heated, and neither to Government nor Opposition encouraging or satisfactory. This untoward event may sometimes occur in the best whipped House of Parliament, and no less in a family of unimpeachable social distinction where the Fifth Commandment is forced under glass to abnormal dimensions.

The Opposition's cheeks were very pink, it had ruffled its pretty hair, its mouth was set and in its prolonged study of its bronze shoes was no sign of submission. The Government looked ominous.

Yet upon the whole, the Countess von Vallade deemed it imprudent to insist farther at the moment. Nothing permanent could be done, she was well aware, until Eck Flemming was gone. His temporary absence was well, but only his final departure from the country could render Nelka pliable. It was best without many words to let things proceed little by little and close up round her until she was

too involved and confused to extricate herself.
That had been the countess's opinion from
the first, and she had not hesitated to urge it;
but Baron Frege unwisely insisted upon too
frequent soundings. The man was impatient.
Well — his age hardly warranted prolonged
delay. He wanted Nelka — yes, undoubtedly;
but — it was policy to scan the whole field —
there were other candidates and enough of
them, and whom his suave sister really favored
was by no means clear.

Then Nelka's pointed indifference might any
moment offend him beyond reparation. Her
manner to him was becoming really quite abominable. Up to this time she had seemed marvellously unconcerned or incredulous — at any
rate indisposed to regard the matter seriously.
To-day, and in a less degree more than once
recently, she had been roused, indignant, stubborn, — to call things by their names. The
lady feared, indeed, she had but strengthened
by repeated exercise her daughter's power of
resistance.

There sat Nelka for the first time in her life
unmalleable, unfilial. She had just remarked,
in the clearest possible tone, that Baron von
Frege was a painted mummy, that she loathed

him, and that any suggestion of her marrying
him was simply crazy. There in the secret-
drawer lay Frege's letter. There too was
Benno's last — a fateful juxtaposition in truth!

Benno was truly outrageous; Knod hardly
better; and even Waldemar seemed to be somewhat beyond his depth. Poor boys! They
ought of course to have all they wanted. It
was too absurd they ever should feel cramped.
Still they might be a little more considerate of
their own family. And Eck — why had he
not Frege's money? For Eck was charming.
There could be no doubt of that. The last
time he had spoken earnestly with her, he was
so manly, so persuasive, so reasonable in his
preposterous schemes, even she for a moment
almost sailed blissfully out of sight of stern
reality, and barely retained sufficient presence
of mind to arrange that at least while his
appointment was pending he should say nothing definite to Nelka; and he had not spoken,
nor had he written, of that the countess had
reason to be perfectly sure. So they had
parted the best of friends, which was a real
comfort, for she was hardly less fond of him
than of her own sons, and none could say she
had made any perceptible difference between

them and him when the four children were together. Why, she even used to kiss him good-night in his cot-bed quite the same as Waldemar, and year after year in the holidays see the strange child's dark locks and her own boy's fairer head almost on one pillow. No, her conscience was tranquil on that point.

Nor was she one of those heartless cynics who systematically discountenance love-matches. On the contrary she approved of consulting the affections whenever it was feasible. She herself, when she married Erich, had been quite as pleased and silly and all that as any girl, and was very fond of him still of course, and all that. Certainly she had been an excellent wife to him, and it was considered everywhere an unusually happy and united marriage. And Erich thirty years gone had been the veriest Romeo. Why, Aunt Clotilde even thought he acted almost *bourgeois*. Still marrying for love was not all of life, or why was she so worn with heavy care; trying to the best of her ability to serve her family's interests, yet to all intents and purposes struggling on alone? In really vital matters, how much support and sympathy had she from Erich now, in spite of his raptures then?

Bad as things were, did she so much as intimate a remedy, he invariably said, and sharply
too, for lovers' voices change a bit in thirty
years, " For God's sake, don't worry the child!
Hurry her in nothing. Let her take her time,
and be happy in her own way," and then he 'd
run his hand with that abrupt motion through
his hair, as if he were on the point of going
distracted if he heard another word. She
dared not show him Benno's letter — so soon
again after the last. One could hardly answer for the consequences. Sometimes indeed
Erich was so terribly nervous and jaded she
feared he would break down altogether.

No, it was but too obvious that young
people's most fulminating emotions could in-
sure no perennial bliss. For her part she
simply held there were occasions when a marriage established on a solid and purely reasonable basis should be welcomed and sagaciously
furthered, and this was distinctly one of them.
Had Eck Frege's millions, she was liberal
enough to prefer Eck, untitled as he was. But
unhappily one could not readjust these things.
One could but accept such facts as Providence
presented and make the best of them. That
is what she intended to do.

Certain miseries of her own experience she would, if possible, avert from that ungrateful child whose downcast eyes and persistent twirling of one blue tassel seemed to proclaim no surrender. Should then a creature so youthful still that she could consume six chocolate éclairs in swift succession, without a symptom of indigestion, be permitted by sane people in cold blood to be the arbiter of her own destiny.

And what, when all was said, did Nelka want? She knew not herself. She had no definite ideas. She simply thought, in her silly school-girl way, it would be nice to go off with Eck on a sort of perpetual picnic. Paul and Virginia! Now what did that mean? In spite of Eck's brilliant mental endowments and will-o'-the-wisp great projects, what in plain words was the position which he, aided by Erich's influence, was moving heaven and earth to procure? That of a mere secretary to a wild horde of explorers and savants. To this amiable nomad Nelka should engage herself, and wait years probably until he could support her. In this visionary fashion he reckoned differently of course, and foresaw mellifluous chances; but how about those two

sisters for whom even now he had to provide
something-a-year?

Nevertheless, according to his naïve pro-
gramme, when he should deign to beckon,
Nelka was to desert her family and station and
to start — on a wheel, in a balloon, anyhow —
with him for unknown parts. While he was
penetrating jungles and making literature, she
would be hanging about fever-stricken ports,
and, like an adventuress, living alone in cheap
pensions, provided they had pensions in Africa,
which was by no means sure. Or would she
go jungling too — a pistol in her belt?

The countess drew herself up, smiled an
Olympic smile, and hoped she knew her duty.
There were ineptitudes too insensate to admit
of discussion — outside an asylum. That nice
little round black head persisted in thrusting itself among her thoughts and pleading
dumbly. It gave her a curious discomfort,
against which she rallied, and feverishly wished
it, with appurtenances, would accelerate its
plans, recede from civilization, and in due
season vanish altogether beneath African skies,
— a sunstroke, a lion, or something, — of course
without hurting him.

"Perhaps we'd better dress now, dear,"

she said affably; "you will wear your brown
velvet, I presume?"

Nelka looked up, and stopped twirling her
tassel.

"I'm not going, mamma," she said reso-
lutely.

"Not going!"

"Not to another one of Baron Frege's
lunches," she declared — inscribing in her
mental agenda, "at least while Eck is away,
and writes me not a word, and everybody and
everything make me miserable."

"This is not Baron Frege's lunch, dearest."

"Well, his sister's then; it is quite the same
thing."

"But we have accepted."

"You — not I."

"But, Nelka —"

"Say anything you like to them, mamma.
If you tell them I don't feel at all well, it is
quite true. The mere thought of the man
makes me seasick. Besides, papa told me last
night I need not always go out if I do not
like. He said there is no earthly reason
why I may not stay at home whenever I
please."

"I am sorry you thought it necessary to

trouble your poor tired papa with such trivial matters," the countess said very sweetly.

Nelka colored.

" I know papa is always dead tired. I suppose it was selfish of me to bother him, though it was only a moment. But some-times — sometimes I don't know what to do or where to turn," she said low and strenu-ously.

This was one of the remarks which the countess thought best not to hear.

" By the way, Nelka dear, — it may be an old-fashioned notion, but at least it is a well-bred one, — I was taught when I was young that when a man loved a woman and offered her his hand and heart, he was paying her high honor, the highest in his power, and therefore, whether she accepted him or not, she was bound to treat him with respect."

"It sounds all right," returned the young girl, slowly; " but somehow there is some-thing the matter with it somewhere." After a moment, " For my part, I think it funny," she remarked disdainfully. " If I see a peach on a tree and want it, should the peach be grateful? To be sure, in some cases — " she reflected, with a marvellous change of expression, but broke off with a sharp, "Besides, nobody has asked me to marry him, and never shall, if I can help it," which was not, in the phrasing at least, strictly accurate.

"Well, well, child, I merely made a suggestion. Let it pass. But I really would not drag my poor father into my petty personal concerns," pursued the mother, gently, "whether I did or did not lunch out."

"Very good," Nelka returned coldly, her gaze steady.

"She is fairly at bay. Never have I seen her so curious," mused the countess, and remarked easily : —

"I shall go, of course, and I am sorry to go alone. Still it is not worth further discussion. What do you propose doing?"

"I intend to learn to make a *bisque*," Nelka returned, with sustained and childlike defiance; "and I am going instantly out to the kitchen to ask that nice little thing to teach me."

Her mother, after contemplating her an instant, rejoined : —

"By all means, my love," but sighed with deep-drawn impatience when the young girl had closed the door behind her.

Presently Nelka returned.

" There, mamma! I made her come. Look at us."

Comtesse Nelka wore a bit of white fluting on the top of her head, had donned a long white apron, pushed up her sleeves, and stood at ease, her arms akimbo. Her expression was brilliantly happy and amiable if a trifle mischievous.

" Ah, Vroni, good-morning," said the lady, urbanely. " You are going to give Comtesse Nelka a lesson? That is very nice I am sure."

" But look, mamma. See me, see us!"

The mother smiled blandly, without regarding her wayward daughter's masquerade. All should be granted her, — caprices, eccentricities, nonsense, luxuries, dainty toilettes they could ill afford. She should perceive and feel their devotion, their self-sacrifice, their boundless indulgence. In return, — she should do her duty.

" Your dinner last night was again perfection, Vroni," she remarked with unwonted benignity and expansion. " Your sauces are so choice; I get nothing so good elsewhere; and that *suprême de pêches* was exquisite. And your accounts always so clear and reasonable.

You seem to get on so quietly with the others
too — you have really conciliated them."

"Oh, dear, yes," Vroni answered with a short
laugh.

"Well, mamma, if you 'll not look at me, —
and I do look nice, — almost as handsome as
Vroni, — I think I 'll go and make my *bisque*."

"Amuse yourself, dear child. I shall not
be gone very long."

Nelka turned on the threshold. "It is not
amusement. It is sober earnest. It is highly
important that I learn to make a *bisque*, you
know, mamma, and immediately."

Now in the comparison deliberately provoked by Comtesse Nelka, and suavely ignored
by her mother, the salient disadvantages ought
to have been on Vroni's side. Appealing to
the comtesse herself for countenance, let us
see if they were.

There are various ways of drawing this comparison. One way is not to draw it at all, to
regard it as non-existent, as did the Countess
von Vallade. Hers was a fine, a subtle way,
and many would do likewise had they her
presence of mind. May their tribe increase
and Allah grant them true vision!

Another way is the way of the *parti pris*

which sits enthroned in estimable craniums,
and categorically judges manners, morals,
tragedies, art, war, crops, politics, hailstones,
and all else under the sun, and is never at a
loss or puzzled, but always burly and cocksure,
because it knows beforehand with no doubt,
study, or examination how all things ought to
be and therefore are.   A comtesse — *pur
sang* — and one of the *prolétaire;* aristocrat,
plebeian ; lady, cook ; delicacy, coarseness ; no
more to be said.   Peace be with them of this
mind also, — and true vision.

But some, wandering over land and sea, not
always in fair weather, and beholding " cities
of men and manners, climates, councils, gov-
ernments " — some no less who stay quietly at
home — have been taught, chiefly, no doubt,
by their own great blunders and frailties, after
much stumbling and groping in the dark, after
sorrow and disaster, to cease forever from drawing hard lines of demarcation between classes,
between soul and soul, and are learning it is no
use to box up and label wares so fluctuating
and protean as human attributes, since they
deride classification, interpenetrate, and law-
lessly spring at one from the wrong box.

For such nomad spirits, they who make

weary pilgrimages, they too who in the body
abide at home, see strange and puzzling sights :
vacuity clad in ermine; kings hauling cod or
tending cattle; a fishwife's face and voice beneath a duchess's coronet; a lady, gentle and
punctilious, crying her wares on the market;
youth, skeptical, astute, and miserly, — age,
ardent, full of faith; the tiger and the ape
stalking in evening dress in Drawing-rooms
and West End clubs; vulgarity, blatant in exclusive cliques where most decried; mixed
motives everywhere; everywhere flung broad-
cast among high and low God's fair gifts of
beauty, brain, and goodness; everywhere the
longing, struggling hearts of humanity, and in
every human heart the base and the divine.

Such seeking pilgrims then who once have
looked thus into the world's kaleidoscope can
no longer extol mere rank, or arrogantly hold
that in the increase of wealth, trade, and in-
vention of machinery lies progress. Without
reviling of that which had in the past its *raison
d'être*, they are inclined to believe that while
the dominant conditions of worldliness and
class privileges endure, civilization has hardly
dawned upon the earth. With longing and with
confidence, they look toward no millennium

indeed, yet to a coming age when the mission
of the slow, inevitable years shall be accomplished; when a sane and wholesome mode of
life and education shall be possible for all,
surrounding all, free as the sunlight and green
grass; when every man and every woman shall
have at least a fair start, a chance, at least, of
attaining his highest possible development;
when public sentiment shall honor the worker
and regard chronic idleness in either sex as a
social disgrace; when woman shall be her own
calm guardian; when prisons, slums, and
brothels, which now attest our cruelty and
cowardice, shall be as obsolete as the rack, the
thumb-screw, the *oubliette*, and all *droits de
seigneur;* when the nations shall have ceased
to be armed bands of barbaric warriors; when,
in short, our apathetic senses shall be quickened
and illumined until we perceive the vital truth
that, however puny and impotent man may
remain before the vast forces of nature, as
regards his own species he is eternally responsible, irrevocably his brother's keeper.

Pilgrims of this complexion — to them, too,
peace and true vision, but true vision at any
cost though peace fail — have then gently
abandoned certain hoary social fictions, have

ceased unquestioning to bow the knee to convention, legend, and tradition, yet duly esteeming these last in their place; and not unmindful all are significant, many indeed beautiful and pathetic relics marking *étapes* on the stern and weary road our brave race has trod in its interminable ascent.

They, the misguided pilgrims, approaching in their own spirit the comparison above proposed, would, with sufferance, employ also their own method, — which some indeed deem dangerously levelling and foreshadowing universal disintegration, — namely, to inspect the two young human creatures as they stand, observe them with fairness, take careful measurements — physical and so far as possible moral — and honestly to record the results — as follows:

VIII

BLUE blood, according to popular credence, should have coursed through the smaller hands and feet; but, as it happened, Nelka's were the longer, larger, and less firmly knit. Vroni should have had the few freckles which did no injury to Nelka's beauty, but high life had monopolized them. The two were not unlike in general coloring, that of Vroni being warmer, more vivid. In height and shape they were not widely dissimilar; but Vroni's bearing was the more resolute and spirited, Nelka's at times somewhat languid — which in her circle was regarded as a grace, but in Vroni's would have been denounced as " dawdling."

As to the thing we vaguely term refinement, of which happily are innumerable kinds, beside the special sort monopolized by society news-columns, neither face possessed the refinement which profound thought may impart, or that of patient sorrow, or of certain forms of ill

health, or that which the habit of pure and
ardent prayer may lend to the homeliest features; but, so far as smooth fresh faces, like
young children's unetched by emotion and
care, may express refinement, and surely this
must be but in prophecy, one girl equalled
the other, and whether comtesse or cook was
the prettier would be a mere matter of in-
dividual taste. Both had rather large, handsome, pleasure-loving mouths. Both were
by nature careless and frank of mien. But
it must in justice be said for Comtesse Nelka
that, considering the massive disadvantages of
her environment, she was an exceedingly fresh
simple-hearted girl with little nonsense about
her.

In point of education, if by that we mean
the training of one's faculties, Vroni was far
and away beyond Nelka. The little comtesse
could, it is true, chatter in four languages.
She could sing small songs fairly well, knew
who Ibsen was and Tolstoi, but was not
allowed to see *Ghosts* on the stage, or read
the *Kreutzer-Sonata* or *Anna Karenina*.
Sudermann's *Heimath* also she might not
see played, although she and all the young
girls of her set went placidly to *Don Giovanni*,

Rigoletto, and *Traviata*. She never puzzled her little head about these discrepancies in social rubrics, and that was wise, for the great panjandrum himself cannot explain them. She attended art lectures, and was taken to picture-galleries. She read whatever books her mother thought proper for an eighteen-year-old girl in the best society. They were not many, and notably few were written by great authors. Authors have an unpleasant way of sometimes seeking to approach the essential meanings of life.

Nelka could dance admirably. When she made her reverence before their Majesties, she sank down and backward and back and downward, until it seemed impossible for her ever to come up again without touching her fingers to the floor, and what she did with all her mechanism while thus mysteriously poised, you could not imagine, unless she "telescoped" it in some marvellous fashion. At all events, a large portion of her seemed to vanish altogether. Then, boneless as a wave of the sea, yet with the wave's soft solidarity, her eyelids demurely drooping, a half smile on her lips, she floated up again with a serene swan-like

motion and stood erect and suave, none of
her charming person missing. It was a
pretty sight, and a score of lieutenants would
ride hard to see it, and never failed when they
got half a chance, and much good it did
them, for Nelka von Vallade's destiny was an
open secret.

But this one perfect achievement hardly
equipped fair Nelka for the struggle for life.
Thrown upon her own resources, wrecked
upon the immortal desert island of fiction,
flung into the midst of a new and struggling
community, or simply required anywhere to
earn her bread and shelter without aid or
favoritism, it is to be feared she would have
starved. She could ride tolerably well. If
desert islands, struggling communities, or the
haunts of poverty could have provided trained
saddle horses and paid her for looking be-
witchingly pretty on them, she might have
made a fortune. She could skate and cycle, and
was a fine healthy girl and no doll. But they
had stunted her powers curiously, taught her
to do nothing at all thoroughly, and all that
she did was overpraised. Not even those much
spoiled urchins, Benno, Knod, and Waldemar,
were, in their schooldays at least, commended

for what they could not do, — that insult seems
to be reserved for girls, — but were forced to
do solid work for implacable masters who
took themselves and Greek and Latin prose
with unpardonable seriousness, and relentlessly
rubbed mathematics and other *injuriæ* into
the boys' reluctant pates. That there were
a few things not with impunity to be trifled
with, the three learned in their youth, whatever their world took pains to teach them
afterward.

  •   But nobody really minded very much which
way Nelka's accents turned. Gracious and affa-
ble, she sat in the class-room and let professors
parade miles of 'ologies and 'isms before her.
Her vapid themes received flattering marks,
and the master always touched up her drawing. A professor, pointing out to his class
the distinction between true nobility and the
modern paltry sort created through great
wealth or some other inadequate reason,
turned to her and said: "But you, comtesse, with your great and historic name, may
well be proud," etc. Nelka was not silly, but
for an instant felt as if she personally were the
Palladium of the Empire. It was all very
agreeable.

A maid sewed for her, half dressed her, hung up what she carelessly threw down, kept order for her, or there would have been none. Her hands were for the most part pretty and useless appendages like ribbons on her frock. She was presented at Court at the age of sixteen, and had been exceedingly occupied ever since with multitudinous social functions. In spite of her helplessness, due to neglect of certain faculties and to a systematic swathing and compressing treatment of other ones, Nelka was an intelligent being who, had they let her go off and rough it with Eck Flemming, might, inspired by love and under the wholesome influence of necessity, have yet come to her own as an efficient being. Loving and loyal the girl was, a miracle of freshness among things hollow and insincere.

When Vroni made her courtesy, — *Knix*, she called it, — she just touched her toe to the ground behind her, and bending the knees gave a sudden little dip, — a simple process but good of its kind. She could dance after the fashion of Hexenfels. She could sing better than Nelka, if the truth were known, though only folk songs — no *Solfeggi di Bordogni*, no *bianca luna* or *biondina bella*. She liked pictures better perhaps than did Nelka, and coming from market always stood a few moments, her basket on her arm, in the crowd before two broad windows, and had her own clear impressions, which she would not have hesitated to express to the King, had his Majesty given her the opportunity; while Nelka, frank child as she was, yet felt conscious there was a picture-jargon she had not mastered, and dared not always like the thing she really liked. In point of dense ignorance of art there was little to choose between them. But Vroni looked sharply at painted trees and animals, and was quick to perceive anomalies. She knew nothing of great authors; but then all that Nelka knew of them was that they were something for the most part to be avoided by girls of the best society. Vroni had not Nelka's vocabulary and polite phrases, but spoke the Rough Alp dialect pleasingly, not without a piquant charm, sometimes with a faint transmission of the soft tones Dionysius the weaver had caught in Vienna, sometimes with a robust brusqueness rather startling to the nerves; but her audience usually deserved it.

The peasant girl filled ably a position which, beside skill, demanded judgment, fidel-

ity, energy, self-reliance, and many other qualities of which Nelka, for no fault of her own,
rarely displayed a trace. Nor was it Nelka's
fault that she was continually imagining she
required incredible finery, and spending insensate sums, while Vroni, with a minimum of
needs, sent nearly every penny she earned to
Dionysius the weaver, — which was well, for
he was weaving less and less. Certain austere
colleagues of his were busying themselves in
his affairs. Lachesis held his life-thread
loosely. Atropos had raised her shears.

Had the world demanded no more cooks,
did chemists already concoct our nutriment,
Vroni would not have been thrown out of
employment. She could have turned to any
one of a dozen serious occupations. She
sewed well and easily, made for the most part
her own clothes, and regarded it as nothing;
was deft and shrewd in turning and piecing,
and faultlessly and swiftly neat, holding all her
belongings in their appointed order. No domestic work was difficult for her, no farm
work or running or any amount of physical
exercise. She possessed intimate knowledge
of the care of vegetables and domestic animals.
She used ordinary tools like a boy, and hav-

ing none would, like him, have constructed
rude substitutes. Placed in some unimagined
situation where none of her useful arts were
available, she still would have been wholly
unembarrassed, for her energy, combativeness,
elasticity, and mastery of things were trained
powers upon which she could depend.

Concerning what goes by the name of goodness or innocence, by which many mean complete ignorance of certain phases of nature,
these two eighteen-year-old girls stood, it
must be admitted, upon diametrically opposite
ground.

Neither felt within herself any special incentive to probe mysteries. But Vroni had
met rugged facts face to face, yet had been
spared a cynical or even frivolous interpreta-
tion of them; while Nelka in one sense unin-
formed, had yet far more knowledge of the
world — the phrase being used here in its
accepted sense, knowledge of evil, although
why it should not occasionally include knowledge of good is difficult to grasp — than the
girl of the people. For many things are revealed, above all revealed in a false light, only
through their pointedly enforced avoidance.

Nelka was so scrupulously guarded, so con-

tinually instructed what she must not read, or
see, or hear, or understand, or ever seek to
penetrate, she involuntarily scrutinized these
immense precautions and wondered what lay
beyond the Chinese wall encompassing her.

What she knew of the sacred theme of
motherhood — tabooed to young girls of the
best society — was gleaned from chance hints,
repressed smiles, half-spoken sly witticisms
and innuendoes, even though she herself at
sixteen had been publicly proclaimed, with
customary rites, a full-fledged aspirant for
matrimony.

Since with the best will in the world it is
not humanly possible for girls not congenital
idiots to preserve their minds the egregious
blank which certain circles insist they should
simulate, Nelka and her mates perceived much
in the forbidden field.

Novels, for better or worse, abetted this
branch of education. Operas which she might
see because " it was only music," but to the
plots of which it would have been shocking to
allude, lifted portions of the veil. Great Wag-
ner, in ways unsuspected by the authorities,
was perhaps, with the humble exception of
honest Eck Flemming, the one true apostle

of the unknown Eros that had ever crossed her path. For the Master's titanic themes and pulsating tragic figures moved her to vague awe and reverence of the vast elemental forces which the genteel influences encircling her, the fatuous conspiracy of silence no less than frivolous jest and sneer, strove to belie or to belittle.

Curiously enough Vroni also when very young was screened much after the conventional mode of the upper classes. Such solicitude on the part of the peasants living intimately with their hoofed allies may be viewed with more or less incredulity, but is nevertheless a fact. Dionysius the weaver told his child quite as many arrant falsehoods as a person of the finest susceptibilities in the most rarefied worldly atmosphere ever concocted for his. Small new arrivals in the village were, if human, invested with fabulous and mythological ancestry; if of alien race, were ostensibly bought somewhere. The weaver punctiliously assured his little daughter that he had brought home the newborn calf in his sack, and, sure enough, the corroborating bag never failed on such occasions to lie ostentatiously by the door-stone.

On a certain Christmas Eve, or rather Christmas Day, for it was already three o'clock in the morning, Vroni was suddenly roused from sleep. Ordinarily no witch-wind or thunderclap could wake her. But they had had their bit of Christmas tree adorned with candle stumps and a few apples and nuts; had exchanged their simplest gifts of needed woollen things, snuff, shoes, and aprons; had stood gravely before the lighted tree and sung in unison at the beginning and close of their celebration the sweet and touching strains of *Heilige Nacht;* and the deep charm of the festal season, the glamour of the day, had sent her to bed in a state of rapturous excitement. Sleep had rest but fitfully upon her eyelids, and in her happy visions she beheld waving dream-lights, and heard dream-voices chanting always the familiar Christmas hymn.

Not quite sure of the actuality of the unusual sounds and movements which had disturbed her, she slipped into her frock and ran to the kitchen. She was, it seemed, really awake, for a light stood on the table; a great fire was crackling; in the chimney corner lay, in a broad basket, two newborn calves too weak to stand and covered

warmly with old sacks; while Agathe, in
immense agitation, tears streaming down her
cheeks, was tending them better than if they
were human twins, and feeding them from the
flask and tube once Vroni's own. The astonished child lingering with great dazed eyes in
the doorway, the mother curtly requisitioned
her.

"Step along quick, thou starer, and hold
this bottle," and flew forthwith to the barn to
lavish upon the chief sufferer the care and attention of which she was in sore need.

Presently Dionysius also came in from the
cow-mother. Agathe, as she sprang to and
fro, moaned aloud in pity for the brindle,
the feeble offspring, and for the loss to her
own estate, and arraigning fate, repeatedly
vociferated, —

"But 't was a fine big calf I wanted! Woe
is me! *Oh Weh!*"

Although she heated milk six times for
those frail twins, and fed them from the
bottle, and kept them snug and warm, the
little things lived only through holy Christmas Day, and when they breathed their last,
Agathe wept with loud lamentation. But,
thanks to her devotion, the cherished brindle

recovered fully, and when first able to issue from the stall, that she might break no leg or horn or any other evil befall her after her professional troubles, she was respectfully proffered, as she crossed the threshold of the barn, a piece of bread strewn with holy salt, — specially blessed in the church on Candlemas Day for the rehabilitation of bovine mothers, if members of Christian families.

But early on that Christmas morning as the child Vroni, half-dressed, her eyes still big with amazement, sat on the floor by the crackling fire of fagots and pitifully tended the helpless calf infants, Dionysius dropped upon a stool close by and watched her silently.

Suddenly, in her quick way, the girl looked up : —

"Say, father, didst bring them this time in two sacks? Why didst thou buy so weak ones and weak-legged? Yet they are dear. I like them rarely well, better indeed than the last calf thou didst fetch, though he was strong, and stood on his four legs and looked at me. Say, father, what ails Brindle?"

Perhaps Dionysius gazing down upon the basket saw nothing radically iniquitous therein.

He may, too, have dreaded the harsh effect of the half distraught Agathe's realistic ejaculations. It may be his little maid, crouching there with wise and motherly mien, appealed to him in some tender way as herself a woman-child, or he felt reluctant to fib on holy Christmas Morn.

At all events, he abandoned the whole brood of conventional fables, — sacks, storks, rose-bushes, and cabbages, — and gently told her certain truths about the baby-calves, the brindle, — beasts, birds, trees, flowers, and herself. She listened gravely, as children do, hardly astonished, in no wise discomfited, but calmly fitting what he said to anterior matters half-noted, confusing, which now grew clear.

That day at church she looked with softer eyes upon the Manger, and better understood Father Aloysius's simple and tender picture of the Infant Christ among the animals. All day long her mother and she, and the weaver no less, were ministering to the poor things that had not strength to live. It was a bitter grief to her to see them die.

From that time, in her sentiments toward any helpless new-born thing, human or otherwise, and toward the simple marvellous fact of birth, floated, like sacred incense, memories of the weaver's gentle revelations of the universal laws of life upon this planet; memories of her mother's unfailing goodness to animals; thoughts of the Child in the Manger, and great soft eyes like Brindle's gazing at Him from dusky places; and with this, inevitably commingled, the vivid remembrance of those scarce breathing forms in the basket, and the appeal of their great helplessness for pity and protection. Thus, for her, over the whole mystery of birth hovered a Christmas consecration.

Nor did the subsequent rude obviousness of farm-life, the manifold sequence of wholesome natural events which at times frankly but briefly monopolized the attention of the family, ever obliterate those early and powerful impressions.

IX

LESS adroit than a little child in humble families, Nelka stood rather awkwardly handling dishes and implements, dropping things, and soiling her apron.   Her aspirations *bisque*-wards she had been obliged temporarily to curb, because Vroni, although most eager and disposed, could not evolve crabs from her inner consciousness.   But, radiant to have her lovely lady close at hand, companionable, and imploring to be taught something as fast as possible, Vroni had set her the task of mixing a mayonnaise, — a simple thing, yet one made of ingredients that refuse to combine at haphazard.

"Is it very useful, Vroni?" asked the little comtesse, anxiously.   "For instance, on long journeys?"

"It is a thing one has to know, if one knows anything at all," pronounced the high Court of Appeal.

Whereupon Nelka, with the rapt air of a templar vowing himself to a crusade, began to stir, repeating in a painstaking and childlike way her instructions: " Drop by drop, drop by drop," but failing so signally in the enjoined frugality that Vroni soon had to rescue and sustain the imperilled mixture.

" Why do you slowly twirl the plate with the other hand?" asked the comtesse. " Does that make it come faster? "

Vroni looked up slightly surprised.

" I never thought why," she returned. " My master did it,"— for her a supreme reason. Finishing the mayonnaise, she scraped it into a glass, which she set away in the pantry, meanwhile whistling between her teeth a vaudeville chansonette; and as she carefully wiped the mouth of the oil bottle, and whisked it across the range of her olfactories, she unconsciously cocked her left eyebrow with a delightfully ironical expression, — Giraud's inveterate greeting and farewell to that indispensable but uncertain friend.

Nelka watched her with ever-increasing respect, a sort of fascination, and more depressed than she cared to own.

" Now what else shall I teach the gracious

comtesse?" asked Vroni, alert, as if they had already accomplished wonders.

"Perhaps I'll not work any more at present," the young lady returned in her kind way, but quite fine and self-contained, and continued serenely: "I think I shall learn quite as much by looking on. Shouldn't you think that would be a very good way?"

Vroni knit her brows to consider what was to her a wholly novel scheme, and shook her head dubiously, as she fetched a couple of large bowls and mechanically began to scrape salsify.

"Do you stand up always at such work?"

"No, but I know my manners," rejoined Vroni, in this respect somewhat unduly proud.

"But I do not mind at all."

"Nor I," said Vroni, calmly, and sat down, working some minutes in silence.

"You do think I can learn the *bisque?*" burst plaintively from Nelka.

Most reluctant in this special case to disappoint or wound, too honest to flatter, moved also by an instinct steadily and strongly developing in her now, that bade her hold her culinary lore high and intact, yet more than half divining the source of the comtesse's sudden ardor and persistency, Vroni was frankly at a loss what to reply.

"Don't you think I can learn anything at all?" came now quite piteously from the comtesse's lips.

"Not to-day, not very fast," returned Vroni, candidly, but with a curious, motherly indulgence for the other's limitations. "How, indeed, would that be possible? The gracious comtesse takes it not amiss; I cannot lie, and if I did," she added with a bright laugh, "'twould be no use at all, for the oven never lies, and flour, meat, and vegetables tell the plain truth to all the world, and blab how they've been handled."

"I'm afraid so," acquiesced Nelka, dejected before the stern incorruptibility of inanimate objects. To none such had she ever been to school.

"The gracious comtesse," pursued Vroni, her hands deft and swift at her work, "has not the light touch in her fingers."

Nelka disconsolately spread out her long, loose hands on the kitchen table, and looked at them with marked disapprobation.

"Nor does the gracious comtesse know

even the names of things, let alone what hap-
pens when one puts them together."

"No," gloomily assented Nelka; "but the
question is, can I learn?"

"Some things can be taught, some cannot,"
sagely asserted the very rapidly "dawning
colleague" of a great man. "The hand cannot, nor the feeling about things, and the eyes
that see when the back is turned." In quite
unconscious illustration she sprang up, ran to
her range, briskly adjusted some dampers,
moved a saucepan forward and another back,
— all her manipulations rapid in the extreme.
Returning to her employment she remarked
with deep sympathy the tragic hopelessness
of the face she had always seen so radiant
and gay.

"There's a great deal in a knack. Perhaps
there is some other sort of work the gracious
comtesse would have more knack for?"

"I think not, Vroni," Nelka answered quite
simply and humbly.

"There are young ladies that do the click-
click on writing machines in windows."

Nelka shook her head.

"And beautiful shop-ladies."

The comtesse seemed no less disconsolate.

Vroni reflected a while with somewhat mag-
isterial seriousness.

"*Ach was!*" she exclaimed. "The gracious
comtesse shall learn the *bisque* whether or no.
I undertake it, *parbleu!*"

"Oh, Vroni!"

"Ha! 'T would be a blame on us, I'm thinking, if we could not manage a pot of soup!"

"Ah, Vroni!"

"And other things I make no doubt," the
girl declared somewhat rashly, led on by Nelka's
happy animation. "But we'll begin next time
when I can have everything in readiness."

Valiant and encouraged as if she had
already won a medal in her new pursuits,
feeling indeed quite thrifty, diligent, and domestic, the comtesse leaned against the wall
and smiled with sunny benevolence. Vroni
worked steadily on.

"It is pretty here," said Nelka, looking about.
"I had forgotten it was so pretty,—the blue
and white tiles and your shining copper
things, and all." The door was half open
upon the veranda and the January air, though
crisp, was not too chill. "Yes, it is very nice
and fresh and sweet, and polished as a mir-
ror. I shall be coming often now. You'll

get quite tired of me, and I 'm going to learn such a lot."

She gave a little languid sigh from the over-exertion of so arduous a forecast, and resting her head comfortably against the wall, tipped up her pretty chin and stared, with a dreamy smile and pleasing but vague anticipations of the future, at Vroni's graduated and imposing row of ladles.

Vroni, over her prosaic cleaning, scraping, chipping, and cutting, shot quick, adoring glances at her guest.

"It takes rather long to do things, does n't it?" the comtesse remarked amiably.

"Well, they don't exactly do themselves. Salsify is a bit slow."

"Vroni, as I 'm all alone to-day, you might give me my lunch here," Nelka proposed with buoyancy, for the idea savored of doing, daring, and roughing it.

Over a dainty tray and choice morsels to her taste, and in her glad spirit of adventure, she fairly laughed to think how bravely she had rebelled and left the Frege lunch-table in the lurch. She would henceforth always act on these broad bold lines. Besides, Vroni was lovely, — so quaint.

Now and again a head peered into the kitchen and withdrew with respectful promptness.

"'T is rarely like the cuckoo in the clock," Vroni remarked demurely, and both the girls laughed long, finding in each other's merry eyes a well of fresh incentive. Vroni worked on, always in touch with her fiery but discreetly restrained steed, — quietly feeling the bit.

"Why do you run over there so much?"

"Because there are different things going on, and each must have its turn."

"How clever!" returned Nelka, and determined to note that, although what it meant she had not the remotest conception.

Of course she and Eck would live mostly at first in hotels, since he would have to take long journeys, and could not afford a large establishment. She should not mind that at all. In fact she adored hotels. She should not personally ever be obliged to work of course. But it was just as well to understand things, so as to be able to order lovely dinners like Vroni's. Besides, she should not really mind working, Vroni looked so pretty. How charming it would be on some hunting expedition — rather heavy dark-green cloth, short skirt and gaiters, and a Tyrolean hat with cock's feathers was by far the most satisfactory — but she would have to take a lot of thin blouses, Africa was so warm — she did hope blouses would remain in vogue — to surprise Eck with the white cap, and apron, and an easy command of sauce-pans. She wished he could see her now. He would certainly think the cap becoming. He had smiled so beautifully when she was dressed as a Roumanian peasant for the Charity Bazaar.

Dear Eck! If he would only write. Her heart felt a little sore, yet warm and, ah, so tremulously kind. Perhaps a letter was on the way. Probably. Surely. She was so much happier than she had been in many days — without doubt, a presentiment. She often felt something joyful must happen, and it often did. After the *bisque* she would learn to make an *omelette surprise*, it was so delicious and amusing to find the ice in the shell of steaming hot, fruity, creamy things. Eck last time took two big helpings, and, slyly, a third. It would be rather masterly to produce that, say at Ugando, and turn with a smile to Eck. He could bring two or three nice men friends too. Dear Eck!

Meanwhile, Vroni had finished her task, and set away the vegetables to blanch in vinegar. Next she whipped some cream, and put it aside to await its proper place in a complicated dish for dessert. Her movements were swift and gentle. She passed, leaving no trace, not so much as a spoon lying loose. A trifle blunt and droll in her remarks, her smile was warm, and her eyes glowed with delight.

"How did you learn it, Vroni?"

"The gracious comtesse means cooking?"

"Yes, that too. But particularly your nice quick ways of doing things right."

"Fine cookery, my master, at the Schloss taught me. But how to work," Vroni laughed brightly. "Well, I take it 't was my mother's voice. 'T was always after me. Nothing was good enough for it. Nobody worked enough to please it — not I, not my father, not she herself."

"Oh, it must have fatigued you, Vroni!"

"Nay, not so," the girl said stoutly. "It did me but good service. Only oft-times it angered me, for I was always a naughty thing and wild."

With a hearty burst of laughter at some sudden reminiscence she continued : —

"It is a high, clear voice. One hears it far and wide. All the animals know it well. She loves them so, and talks to them, and understands them as does no other, I care not who he be. The gracious Comtesse Nelka would hardly believe how rarely well they love her. Even the pigs had for her other fashions."

"Pigs!" Nelka made a wry face.

"My mother says since the Lord thought well enough of them to make them, they are good enough for her. She says, too, they are clever, and have their own feelings and affections, and are by a long way not so dull and mean as some she knows. 'T is my mother's way of speech. She 'll go on like that by the yard. Truly, after she feeds and talks to them, and gently rubs their backs, I 've seen them play like great kittens, and roll with four feet wagging in the air and seem to laugh, — but only for my mother. And the cows, I could tell tales all the long day how they are friendly with her, and think none be her like. 'T was of such a thing I was just thinking. 'T was a droll sight, and set me

laughing till I wept tears, yet could not stop,
and why I laughed I knew not, nor know now,
for 't was but a simple thing."

With a boyish gesture, she brought down
her fist against the palm of her hand in merry
commemoration.

"Gracious Comtesse Nelka will understand
't was a fine sunny day in the field, and my
mother and I were raking and stacking the
hay, and my mother, as I said, has a clear,
high voice and loud, and to be heard everywhere far and near, and all day long until it
stops at night. 'T was going bravely that
day by the sunny weather, talking east and
talking west, and calling to neighbors all
over the place, for all the women were out,
and as far as one could see, were red and blue
kerchiefs bobbing over the hay. And graz-
ing in the pastures a long distance off on the
other side, were the cows of the whole village, with the hired herdsmen — boys mostly.
And our cow heard my mother's voice, and
sprang away across five fields and three ditches,
and stopped short at my mother's side, and
stood stock-still and looked at her quite sensi-
bly and neighborly, as if just waiting for her
to pass the civil word about the weather.

When my mother turned, she was amazed, and stared and laughed. Then she spoke gently: "Go back again, thou saucy one. I want thee not," and gave the cow a little slap upon the shoulder, and back she went all that long way. But I had such giggles that my work was naught, and my mother chid two hours on the stretch, and till I die I think I must ever laugh when I remember me of that cow's face."

"How lovely the life must be there!" said Nelka with enthusiasm, recalling pastoral effects at the theatre, *Martha* and *L'Ami Fritz*.

"Truly," Vroni assented with a warm home feeling. "'T was our little brindle," she added, after a moment. "To be sure she had good reason to like my mother, who once saved her life, when she was in a sore strait by her first calving. No other care except my mother's could have pulled her into shape — but after that she was a thrifty bearer."

"Indeed," remarked the little comtesse, astonished but very polite, after which she was silent for a while.

"It was not too hard work in the fields,

Vroni? Too rough? Did it not tire your back?"

"Oh, if it's not one sort of work, it's just another," Vroni returned, with cheerful philosophy; "but, *Gottlob*, 't is never one sort, and no change. Of course, our kind must work. Why, I suppose, did we not work, we'd starve, although I never thought of that before. Comtesse sees we know no other sort of life. To our kind life is work. I cannot think how it would feel, always to make holiday. 'T would not much please me for sure. Field-work I always liked. Of aching backs, I know naught, but not a little of aching heads. Surely 't is less hard than that dark factory, that looks as if it must have foul smells. I am at home where great winds blow. I could not live cooped up or lolling either, if the gracious Comtesse Nelka takes it not amiss."

With a certain breezy strength she swung a heavy kettle off her range, and over to a corner from whence, stooping amid steam and meat fumes, she remarked blithely: —

"But 't is a pity all have not my tidy work. Mine is the prettiest for sure," and flung the veranda door further open.

Nelka, becoming curiously thoughtful, watched her quietly, admiring her pretty and sure motions, but wondering most at her systematic forethought, for she seemed to be working far ahead, crushing roasted breadcrumbs, and storing them in a glass jar for something or other on the day after the morrow, and impending oysters of the next week; and while doing each task so completely, performed many a neat little intermezzo, and ever and anon the expert solo on the dampers of that big range, which looked as complicated as a locomotive.

"I never dreamed there was so much head-work in it," sighed Nelka.

"What then? Heel-work?" asked Vroni, flippantly, but waited for no answer, as she had already fetched from her store-room a couple of handsomely browned roast ducks, and with a fine blade began most skilfully to carve them. While doing this exquisite work, she had the habit of silence. Carving was a branch of her art Gireaud had taught her to regard with profound respect, if not with veneration. Nelka, deeply absorbed, followed every turn of the clever wrist, every incision and clean stroke of the steel.

"It's wonderful!" at length exclaimed the comtesse.

"'T is tidy," returned Vroni, frankly pleased. "'T is my master's own way. None other has it, save myself."

Smiling a little roguishly, having laid the bird open, she now proceeded largely to recreate him, until a careless eye would hardly perceive the dissecting lines. Dexterously binding his disintegration with coquettish pink ribbons, she packed him in a hamper, and turned her attention to his brother, whom she likewise unmade and re-made artistically.

"Well!" gasped Nelka.

"They and these other things are for Count Benno," prattled Vroni. "A cosy supper for two was my order," she added innocently, at which Nelka, her eyelids drooping, faintly smiled. "I can venture to send the birds carved, because the white Tiber is coming himself for them, and will hold them with steady hands. He's a queer, shy lad, white Tiber, but good to dogs and willing, and can be trusted with my ducks. Ha! 't is not by all men folk I 'd send them."

Filling a small jar with a currant-red concoction, one of the small battalion she for an

hour past had been guiding simultaneously
toward perfection, she fitted it in a snug corner of the hamper, in which had disappeared
a dish of celery salad, and sundry small and
eligible concomitants, and explained : —

"'T is the Hubertus-Sauce Count Benno
likes so well.   He told white Tiber to tell
me it was *phe-nom-e-nal!*   A stout word that.
I doubt I say it rightly."

"What a bright boy Benno is, to levy on
our kitchen.   He always knew how to help
himself to sweets," Nelka was considering,
together with some other of Benno's idiosyncrasies and vagaries, when Vroni said simply
and serenely : —

"Now, if my gracious Comtesse Nelka
takes it not amiss, I want my kitchen."

The comtesse stared, surprised, and smiled.

"You actually mean to put me out ?"

"'T is like this," Vroni explained, in the
placid strength of her position.   "As Comtesse Nelka knows, I have been doing but odds
and ends of no account."   Nelka's face expressed blank amazement.   "Now, it is time
for work.   My dinner needs my thoughts.
Soon the other servants will be coming in.
Besides, I am composing the menus for two

company dinners, which I ought to submit
to-morrow to the gracious countess. A cook
must now and then be alone with her own
thoughts."

That one moment, could Gireaud have
heard her tone, so convincing in its gentle
dignity, — he who often enough was on the
point of tearing his hair because of her
obtuseness, — it would have outweighed all
his sufferings.

"I will go, Vroni. But I shall come again
very soon. It is the nicest place in the
house, and next time I shall learn a lot."

Vroni held the door open for her.

"I 've liked it rarely well to have the gracious Comtesse Nelka so long with me in my
kitchen," she said slowly, in the soft tones
she had for few. Her eyes were loving.

"You are such a nice girl, Vroni. Such a
dear," Nelka returned, her hand extended.

Vroni stooped quickly and kissed it.

"Next time, Vroni!"

"Next time, gracious comtesse."

That evening the Vallades were, exceptionally, at home and without guests. The
countess after dinner wrote numerous little
notes at her little table, and six pages richly

underlined to Benno.   The count sat in his
study at the moment Nelka hovered upon the
threshold, not writing but motionless, his
head on his hand.

"May I come, papa?"

"Certainly, my darling."

As he looked up, his weary face changed,
for he loved his fair girl dearly, although he
had never taken time to occupy himself much
with her, nor did he in point of fact know her
very well.   He perceived neither her weak-
nesses nor her dormant strength.   He took
his children's characters for granted in a
sketchy way, and felt personally injured when
they disproved the accuracy of his optimistic
preconceptions.

His sons had given his theories sundry
rude shocks, but, after each percussion, he
reassumed approximately his original position.
His daughters had never deranged him.

"What is it, Nelka?" he asked indulgently,
half seating himself on a corner of his table,
and throwing his arm round her.

She nestled in silence against him.

"It must be something very large.   A
frock? A necklace? Out with it," for in
spite of ebb-tide in his fortunes, he usually

tried to arrange matters to please the child.

She shook her head.

"It is not things."

"What then?"

"Do you think I am good for much, papa?"

He laughed incredulously.

"You? Rather! I should say so."

"What am I good for?"

"Good for the eyes, and still better for the heart."

He waited an instant, but as she did not speak, went on pleasantly:—

"Very good to laugh with, and at this moment good to laugh at if you are trying to have the blues — a rôle quite foreign to your character," giving her back a series of encouraging pats.

Still she was silent.

"Good to love and be proud of," he went on with real tenderness. "My dear little daughter, my joy and blessing, the very flower of my home."

Moving slightly she faced him wistfully.

"Is that all?"

"Is it not enough? Are you not glad to be your father's comfort?"

"Of course, papa, but — "

Now Count Vallade's thoughts were occupied with really serious matters. Even as he spoke, he was broadly sketching a paper he was about to draw up, in which he must vindicate and gratify the Government, conciliate the respectable Opposition, enrage no farther the rabid Socialists, and win over if possible the Clerical party, — in short, sit blandly astride the thorny diplomatic hedge. This somewhat lacerating position was his speciality.

It is, therefore, a proof of his kindness and affection, that he had so much patience with his pet's childishness. He would indeed rather see her smile.

Believing that he read the cogitations of the dear head upon his shoulder, he went on : —

"And later, though I hardly dare to think how I shall miss you, you will be some other man's blessing."

"His flower?" murmured the girl to her father's coat collar.

This curious observation, the count was not certain how to interpret, but he repeated with emphasis : —

"His flower! The fair flower he will proudly wear upon his breast."

"A sort of buttonhole bouquet," commented the muffled voice.

He smiled, slightly surprised.

"Has my baby grown cynical? You should not pour cold water on your old father's fancies. At all events it will be a lucky fellow that will get you. You will be his — "

"Sunshine," she suggested, almost inaudibly.

"Well, what else, in a man's stern life, is a lovely girl, a sweet young wife, but pure sunshine? In her presence he lays aside his professional cares. The mere sight of her rests him, amuses, cheers, and entertains him."

"His kitten."

"Oh, come, Nelka!" he remonstrated good-humoredly, "what is the meaning of this? How am I to please you? A woman softens, enriches, warms, and embellishes a man's destiny."

"His fur coat," muttered the stifled voice.

"Yet she is something far above him — something to be kept stainless, untouched by the world's dust and mire."

"The cornice," she remarked, gazing at the ceiling.

"Rogue!"

But he saw her lashes were wet. What a sweet child she was! Not a line on her fair face, peachy like the painting done when she was six years old.

"You are tired, dear," he said solicitously. "I think you'd better go to bed. Besides, I have some rather trying work to think about. Come to me again very soon. Next time we'll have a good talk, and you shall tell me what sort of proclamations you are getting up in that little head."

"Yes, papa. Next time."

He took her in his arms.

"Good-night, my pet. Be happy, and amuse yourself. Leave care to me."

He sighed, and his handsome pale face clouded as he turned to his desk. He ran his hand abruptly through his iron-gray hair.

She stood an instant irresolute, in her heart a dim swarm of nameless thoughts and desires struggling to shape themselves.

"If I might help you to bear it!" she exclaimed fervently.

"Ah!" he returned, not without a trace of

impatience, "how is that possible! Let us be rational, my dear." Then, gently, for in her limpid eyes was grief: "Be sure your father loves you, Nelka."

"I know."

"And if you would help me, be your bright fresh self. Let me feel that when I return home from all sorts of storms and agitations, you are waiting placid, smooth-browed, always the same."

"The mantel-shelf," she said, but this time to herself.

She stood presently by her mother.

"Good-night, mamma."

The countess also smiled affectionately as she glanced up. She too looked tired and worn.

"Good-night, my love."

"Could n't we go into the country?"

"What, in the middle of the winter?"

"No, but some time."

"I don't know what you mean, child. Is not Waldmohr country — and Switzerland?"

Nelka lingered.

"Can I do anything for you, mamma — help you in any way?"

"Thanks, no dear," the lady returned, a

little absently. " Nelka," she said with sudden scrutiny, "aren't you a trifle pale for you? Yours happily is not the sort of skin that goes off early, still the nights we are not on duty I 'd get a couple of hours extra sleep if I were you. And use a little of that last preparation of lanoline. I find it softening."

X

THE broad path winding up the slope of the little park sparkled with new-fallen snow in strong sunshine, and the trees were white. Vroni, returning from early Mass, walked briskly and for entertainment crunched as loud as possible with her stout shoes.

"In Hexenfels we have no such fine paths," she reflected admiringly. "The town gets up bright and early, like a tidy maid. The plough had already been here as I went down. Now I wonder who sees to all the sweeping of the snow."

Musing thus innocently upon the mysteries of municipal housekeeping, she was not unmindful that a person she once casually but pertinently met had knelt beside her and stood at the church porch and stared as she came out.

"A rude fellow with shiny eyes," she calmly labelled him. "'Tis the same man. I remem-

ber me I did give him a good whack.   Ha!
Were it not just now in Holy Church, 't would
have gladdened me to serve the other ear as
neatly, for truly 't is ill-mannered to take more
than one's share of kneeling place, and jostle
elbows when there's room for all to pray to
God in peace."

In hearty and jocund fashion she was devoted to her Church.   Not troubling her head
to meditate upon ulterior meanings, she loved
with joyful and childlike loyalty its prayers,
ceremonies, and symbols, its rich atmosphere,
and most ardently its music.   When she left
her village for the second time, she had begged
for the tarnished gilt Heart pierced with seven
spears,— an emblem which all her life had
hung on the kitchen wall.   Dionysius proposed she should rather take a little waxen
lamb bearing the banner of the Cross, or even
buy herself a fine new blue-and-white Virgin
in the town.   But Vroni insisted upon having
the bleeding Heart and the red rosary of imitation coral beads that hung below it.   She said
wherever she went they would always look
cheerful and homelike.

A step came crunching behind her, a longer,
faster step than hers.   She turned involuntarily

and saw the piano-man, before she remembered her father had warned her an honest maid in town carries her head straight. Now in Hex-enfels it would have been considered unsocial if not proud had one not looked back and passed at least a good-morning where two were treading the self-same path. Slightly vexed that she had recalled his injunction too late, she hastened her pace, but the man's stride gained on her.

Presently Vincenz Berg joined her and po-litely took off his hat.

She gave him one indignant glance, and trudged on sturdily.

" It is a pleasant morning," he remarked affa-ble as any fine gentleman, and flourished a handkerchief with a red border like Count Benno's. The man she saw looked not un-like Count Benno,— pointed moustache, clean cheeks, shiny bold eyes, and all.

Vincenz wore a quiet-colored overcoat as long as Count Vallade's, and was a good-look-ing fellow with an agreeable voice, a ready smile, and exceedingly smooth manners. The latter were in part a natural gift, in part ac-quired in the service of an ambassador whom Berg, some years previous, had accompanied

as valet to St. Petersburg, Athens, and other
distant points, thereby effectually seeing the
world, and enjoying a life of elegant idleness.
Neither the one nor the other happened to be
a specially spiritualizing process, and the com-
bination proved devastating to his facile principles. He was however bright, brisk, and
good-humored enough, an able workman,
drawing and spending good pay, a favorite
with his mates, jovial and prompt at his beer.

Vroni saw no cross path in which she could
quickly spring aside. High snowy shrubbery
bordered the way. Turning back would do
no good. She was averse to taking to her
heels as if she were afraid. There seemed
nothing to do but to go on. Glowing from
the crisp air and inward irritation, her eyes
stormy, she walked with a rapid, resolute step
and looked straight before her.

Vincenz, smiling, greatly admiring her,
twirled his moustache.

" It 's a very good path through the snow,"
he said harmlessly like an old acquain-
tance.

" 'T is not wide enough for two," retorted
Vroni, fiercely.

" Oh ho! " laughed to himself the young

man of large experience. "So this is the kind we are."

"I have seen you so long and often now," he went on simply and pleasantly, "on your veranda, and coming and going, and at church, that I feel I know you by this time."

"But you don't," she flung at him with a scowl.

"Well, I want to awfully, and there's no harm in that I hope," he returned with a laugh. "I'm sure I'm doing my best. My name is Vincenz Berg."

She turned and looked at him squarely, in spite of herself perceived his youthful pleasantness, and was vaguely startled that something within her was pleading for him, while something else distinctly resented his smiling insolence. At the Schloss were men more or less of his sort, she remembered, and how Armand Gireaud used to draw up his face in ineffable grimaces and witheringly pronounce the band jackanapes.

"I know you not," she said grimly, "nor do I want to know a staring man, and a jostling man, and a man that follows honest maids from Holy Church, and a jackanapes and," waxing still stronger with the vigorous sound

of her own voice, " you can go back or you
can go on, for I'll trudge no further with the
like of you, as if we two belonged together.
Ha!" and she stopped short.

"We do belong together," he returned
softly, wholly unperturbed by her oration.
" As to staring, when I see anything as pretty
as you, I have to look, don't I? Would you
have me shut my eyes? And I'm not following you home from church. I happen to be
going the same way, that is all. That's not
my fault, I suppose. How can you be so hard
on a fellow?"

His bold gaze rested insistently upon her.
He was already what he called in love.

" *Saprelotte!* " muttered Vroni, her breathing quick, her nostrils dilating. She looked
helplessly about her for a weapon. A stout
broomstick would have suited her mood.

"Well, I'll leave you the whole path, then,
if I must."

"Go!" she exclaimed, and stamped her
foot.

He took off his hat with an air of quiet and
concentrated devotion, a trick he had caught
from His Excellency, and strode on. She
watched the tall lithe figure climb the path.

At some distance, before passing out of sight behind a group of Norway pines, he turned, dark against the snow, and swung his hat.

" 'T is a jackanapes," she muttered, " and like his impudence to make a soft voice at me and say, ' We two belong together.' "

It seemed to her truly astounding that from that day she hardly moved without meeting Vincenz Berg. Busy upon her veranda, she would assume unconsciousness of his confronting windows, but a subtle telepathy conveyed his ardent messages, and she would frown defiantly while setting milk jugs airing in the sun. Coming from market or from church, she could almost count upon him to cross her path, look intently in her eyes, take off his hat respectfully, and disappear round some corner. Gradually she became so accustomed to his manœuvres that when by chance he failed to appear, in her wonderment was an infinitesimal and wholly indefinable sense of loss.

" The jackanapes, 't is time in truth, he should repent him of his crackbrained swoopings," she would then reflect, her quick exhaustive glance scanning each nook and passage where the monster had ever darted out. She cherished the artless delusion that her demeanor to him was uncompromisingly austere, and never suspected the gleam of merriment her eyes sent forth, or how invitingly her color came and went. For though it was "a blame" to him, and, she honestly believed, to her at first pure vexation, when she found he spoke no more, nor even followed her, but merely dashed out a doorway or round a corner, never twice from the same ambush, his evolutions began to afford her no small degree of excitement and interest. The complete uncertainty of his movements lent to them in her childlike mind the zest of a merry game. Once, indeed, she almost smiled back at his now familiar face peeping over the ample shoulder of her own butter woman at market, but frowned perfunctorily and looked the other way.

Berg's conspicuously romantic behavior began not unnaturally to awaken facetious comment in Vroni's immediate circle, where indeed love affairs, open or surreptitious, were topics no less absorbing than on higher planes. "Vroni's sweetheart" they dubbed him, while he but hovered upon the horizon. Everybody possessed, she had already discoved, a past, present, or potential sweetheart. Beside the servants' affairs of the heart, those of the Comtesse Nelka and the Vallade brothers were exhaustively discussed in her presence; and not without discriminating intelligence. Never having read a novel, Vroni made her own fresh discoveries of trite facts in the vast field which she was beginning to perceive encompassed her on every side.

"Thou, Melchior, what thinkest thou of love?" she began blithely on a Sunday, as the three sat at their four o'clock beer, not as usual in a suburban tavern, but in his house; for he was nursing a cold, together with the aggrieved notion that immunity from vulgar physical ills ought, were things properly managed, to be one of the perquisites of his position.

He assumed a graver aspect preparatory to utterances of weight.

"'T is rubbish mostly," quoth Jakobine.

"But they are all at it," laughed Vroni, "though fairly criss-cross and awry. *Du lieber Gott*, 't is an odd distemper! I'm glad I never caught it. Seest, Melchior, they that would marry have no money, and, should they wed, they 'd lose their situations. I ask thee, is that fair dealing? And there be some love-sick with some that sigh for some that look toward others. Truly I cannot think how that would feel — may be 't is like a pinching shoe. Then, Melchior, so thou be good with one most nice and pleasant-spoken, and kind to men and maids, and strong and comely too, with a high head and clear eyes, thy father and thy mother bid thee wed a grisly one with gold, and though thou canst abide him not at all — 't is most curious! — art thou a most gracious lady, canst do naught to help thyself. Then there are other most strange things and hard to understand. The *Herrschaft* are all for getting married. 'T is the main thing, it seems, for gentlefolks, and there 's much talk and fuss till all the gracious lads and maids be joined unto their gracious mates. The ladies' sweet-hearts come with top hats on, bold as thou willst, in broad daylight. But Franziska Brandt must ever slip out slyly, when all the gracious *Herrschaft* are at dinner, and meet him by the fountain or in the garden corner of the court where 't is pitch darkest. And one of the first things they ever ask of thee is, ' No followers, eh?' in a quite awful voice."

"Art making progress, Vroni," sneered Jakobine.

"'T is time I learned somewhat," the girl replied serenely. "I must ofttimes smile when I remember me how I was ignorant of things, and not so very long ago."

"'T is plain enough whither thy thoughts are flying fast."

"Hast not a sweetheart, Vroni?" anxiously demanded Melchior. "Art not doing us that ill turn?"

"Nay, nay, not I!" but she colored with a slight sense of guilt, for the ubiquitous Vincenz had followed her to her brother's threshold.

"Then talk not thus," Melchior remonstrated.

"How so, brother?"

"So bold and pert," suggested Jakobine.

"So social democratic," warned the king's coachman. "I cannot listen to such talk. Our Club cannot abide it. We are all respectable and very prudent men."

"I doubt it not, but what, pray, has thy great virtue to do with me?"

"Thy ways and tone are free, and please me not," he continued with a disgusted air. "Dost begin by finding fault with thy superiors, willst end by siding with that low and

crazy lot. Wouldst surely lose thy situation —
which would reflect on me."

Vroni stared, and broke into a hearty laugh.
"Nay, Melchior, nay. 'T was not ill meant.
I found no fault. I but idly spoke of things
I see with my own eyes and hear with my own
ears, and that give me pains to fit together in
my mind, seeing they be misfits."

"I could wish thou 'dst ever think of my
position," he returned sulkily.

"*Ach was!*" she cried impatiently, "dost
think thou holdest up the whole palace! Had
I a dozen sweethearts, where were the wrong
to thee?"

He frowned, puzzled, and comprehending
not at all. Jakobine indulged in a chapter
of gloomy prophecies upon the doom of the
light-minded. Vroni, having only them,
promptly regained her temper, and did her
best to re-establish peace. With sunny
smiles she told tales which coaxed reluctant
twitches from even Jakobine's grim lips; recalled home scenes to Melchior until he had
simple and human intervals; proposed to
trim a hat for her sister-in-law, who accepted,
remarking that she, *Gottlob*, had no talent for
vanities; agreed to knit a woollen waistcoat

for her brother, — 't was a new thick stitch she
said, that kept one warm; and left them not
indeed approving, but half mollified by her
innocent wiles. Yet it was uphill work she
felt, as she turned from their door.

Jakobine had not asked her to stay. Jacko-
bine never asked her to stay or to come again.
Jakobine was as frosty to-day as in the hour
they met, and Melchior was putty in her
hands. Vroni on her way to market had occasionally gone straight to his stables. There
among his horses he seemed quite a different
man, so able and so kind — not a bit respectable; but Jakobine was furious when she found
it out, — it was indeed no secret, — and Melchior asked Vroni not to come again, unless
for something urgent and unavoidable, he
added feebly. He had enjoyed her cheery
little visits, and the men were jollier with him
on the days they spied the white apron and
brown basket. Vroni nodded brightly right
and left since, they were all fellow-workmen
of her brother, and it was evident to him she
made a good impression, for even the head-
coachman spoke of her friendly manners and
offered him a glass of beer. But it was no
use to oppose Jakobine. So now they never

met except in her intimidating presence.
Sometimes they telephoned; Melchior was
very nice by telephone. It always gave her
a glad surprise to hear the home voice speaking from the wall.

"Melchior was not to blame for his cold,"
she reasoned, as she reluctantly walked home,
still it was not quite the very worst cold that
ever was in the world. Had he the spirit
to take a brisk walk over the hills, say to the
Hunter's Horn, it would surely do him good.
Ah, the people looked so happy, and the
music was so gay, yet sometimes soft and sad,
and they sang songs that made your heart
beat and little shivers run down your back.
How wonderful to hear that men's chorus
hushing itself in one great, soft, long, sweet
sound. It was heaven. When they stopped,
the whole crowd was still as stone, and drew
its breath before it again began to chatter and
jingle glasses.

It was not happy to come out for one's
Sunday, and turn one's self about and march
home again. Probably she was the only maid
in the whole town who was having no pleasure.
In fact, there could be no doubt of this deplorable circumstance. Of what use was it for

Melchior to muffle himself up as if he were his own grandmother, and sit huddled over the fire, when he would have to be on duty in the morning, as well as go once to the stables that very night? Jakobine probably did it all on purpose. She knew Vroni longed to go to the Hunter's Horn and hear those men sing. If ever she expressed a special wish, Jakobine opposed it if she could. Should Jakobine tell Melchior he was well, from that moment he would not dare to sneeze.

It was ridiculous. For her part she should never marry. She had a poor opinion of marriage, love-making, and all that sort of thing. She should live simply and solely for her profession, as her good Gircaud had strongly advised. All the same, she wished she might have some enjoyment. Sweethearts seemed useful to go about with, at all events. Everybody had friends and occasional gay hours; she knew nobody save Melchior and Jakobine, and they, alas! were never gay.

No, they were emphatically dreary. Still they were her family. If they would be but a trifle friendly, she would be so thankful. Never in her life had she struggled so hard to be civil as to Jakobine, who had not so much as asked her to stay to supper. She wished she might have stayed. After all, Melchior was her brother, if he did mope and muffle.

Bright groups of fathers, mothers, children, and lovers lagging behind, met her. She only was alone. She would go home and begin to knit Melchior's waistcoat. Truly a pretty business for a young maid's free day. She might as well be Tante Ursula. Vroni pitied herself vastly.

But if she could but see her father she would not mind not hearing the chorus at the Hunter's Horn. No, she would miss nothing in all the world. With a real pang of homesickness, her heart yearned for the weaver, and her inner vision saw him vividly, pale and dear in the old familiar clothes.

At that instant Vincenz Berg, handsome, friendly, and debonair, crossed the street and came straight toward her.

" May I not walk a bit with you?" he asked without a shade of arrogance.

" Nay," she replied plaintively. "I must go my way alone."

Without a word he dropped behind, and followed her.

" He also seems to be alone. For sure, he

gives up everything to follow me about. He
goes off gentle as a child when I but speak.
'T is mannerly. Even my father would give
him praise for that. Doubtless he 'd take me
to the Hunter's Horn. Doubtless 't would
gladden him no less to hear the songs. Ha!
'T would but serve my Jakobine right! I
would my father had not bade me make no
friends with strangers in the street, for truly I
fain would laugh and jest to-day. I'm a bit
wild at heart, and could greatly run and spring
and shout, were it not town and Sunday and
I, poor maid, alone."

She sighed and hurried on, ever conscious
of the subtle comradeship of the man's light
step behind her.

"'T is true, he was right ill-mannered at the
Schloss and once again. But that was long
since. Doubtless he repents him sore. He
seems no longer like a stranger. He is
patient, one must say, and minds my word,
and was right glad to see my face. 'T is no
harm surely that he follow me, since he 's no
wolf, but tame and gentle-blooded."

Smiling faintly, she felt no longer lonely, for
that companionable footfall kept rhythm with
her own. She experimented childishly, walk-

ing faster, slower : it met her whim ; it followed her to the gate, where as she turned she could not help giving him one swift side-glance. What it said, she little knew, but Vincenz smiled all the way to the beershop.

XI

FORMALLY off duty, Vroni punctiliously avoided intrusion upon her domain and its viceroy.

"To-day I belong fairly nowhere," she lamented as she found her knitting needles and some wool, and happily meeting nobody, for she felt rather ashamed of her flagrant friendlessness and isolation from all earthly joys, stole into the servants' dining-room, where, if without true resignation yet somewhat comforted and stimulated by the large suggestiveness of her small adventure, she proposed to pass some hours of undeserved solitude.

At the large table beneath the hanging lamp a man in a blue uniform appeared to be writing either with his nose or with the uppermost tuft of his shock of flaxen hair.

"Oh, thou here, Tiber? *Grüss Gott*," she said carelessly; sat down opposite him, and began to take up her stitches.

He started in joyful surprise, pushed his chair awkwardly, half got up as if to salute an officer, grew red, stammered " *Grüss Gott,*" and sat down again. As she said nothing more, but with a half frown steadily regarded her knitting, he shyly resumed his work. For some time nothing by way of social intercourse took place between them, beyond the click-click of her needles, a humble and stealthy glance at intervals from under his white eyelashes, and the angry spluttering of his misused pen.

After a while she deigned to say indifferently, without looking up : —

" What leads thee hither to-day, Tiber? "

He answered with the hesitating thick utterance which at times oppressed him : —

" Count Benno's off somewhere, but late must come to town and dress again for something else, a feasting at Baron Frege's, if I err not. I was to bring his things and wait for orders."

" Truly," she remarked in her novel misanthropical vein, "the plums are poorly measured in the great world's pudding. 'T is all for some, for others none." Yawning a little, she withdrew into the remote region of her thoughts.

At length Tiber's incessant scratching began

insidiously to distract her attention from her great grievances. She peered at him inquisitively, as his heavy hand laboriously traced oblique characters, by turns attenuated and swimming in turbid ink — a vigorous *chiaroscuro*.

"*Na*, Tiber, what dost thou there so busily?"

"Writing," he replied solemnly.

"Writing, for truth! Have I no eyes to see — or ears to hear thee?" she added with a laugh. "*Ach*, Tiber, art a queer lad — but good to dogs. There, I will not chide, since upon the instant thou wearest then thy beaten look. Say, what meanst with thy copy-book and ragtag bits of paper? Dost love to be cooped up on a Sunday and bury thy white head in scribbles? Hast no wishes, man? Knowst no place where are merry folk and laughter and songs that beat like great birds on the wing?"

She sighed, clicking with overcharged swiftness.

"Wishes enough have I," returned the man in his slow way, "yet all one wish." As if fearing his own boldness, he broke off and watched her furtively. Vroni paid no heed.

Slowly and shyly he pushed a heap of scattered leaves across the wax-cloth table-cover.

"Mayst see it, Vroni, if thou willst."

She took up the nearest scrap of paper and read aloud : —

"'A detachment of the enemy's cavalry is approaching across the third bridge over the brook behind the wood to the north of the tower.' *Lieber Himmel!*" Reading one after another of the scattered fragments, "'A detachment,' 'the enemy,' 'the enemy is approaching.' Truly a goodly lot of enemies. *Na!* 'T is a long brook, eh, Tiber? 'The enemy.' Another. More. Hast nigh to thirty enemies, all coming over the bridge at once, and thou that wouldst not hurt a fly! *Ach*, Tiber!"

For some unaccountable reason her rollicking mirth encouraged the diffident man not a little. He rested his arms on the table and stared across at the mischievous face under the little white cap. On his honest features was a broad smile of unutterable friendliness and something more, and his blue eyes sought hers with an insistence at variance with his halting manner and inarticulate speech.

"What meanst thou with these thy enemies?" she demanded imperiously.

"Count Benno set me at it, that I may learn to 'nounce. He says I glare at him and contort instead of simply saying who in the devil wants to see him. The manner of his speech is high for me, but the kernel, 't is clear, is that I please him ill. So I 'm to write it fifty times, and say it then out of my own head and learn to 'nounce."

"*Ätschgäble!* 'T is seemly of him to spring from small roebuck to truffled turkey while thou, sweating I mark well overmuch, dost trot o'er hill and dale his fifty mounted men on a Sunday by fair weather!"

"He gave no orders I should work to-day," the man said mildly. "But having the task on hand, likewise to wait for him, I thus filled up my time. Count Benno is no hard master."

"'T is plain!"

"Truly he is kinder than any ever was to me save my mother and," hesitating an instant, "thee, Vroni."

She looked at him half wonderingly under the strong light, and liked the voice with which he had just spoken, a deeper voice than Vincenz's she observed and less smooth, but

strong, sincere, and pleasant to the ear whenever Tiber forgot to stammer.

" Stand up, Tiber, in thy high boots," she
said presently.

He rose obedient.

" Turn round upon thyself, and slow."

He revolved as on a pivot.

" Again," she commanded. " Walk thither
to the door, once, — twice, — and thrice.
'T is well." She nodded gravely. " Naught
fails thee. A good straight-legged strong
lad. Why then hast fear? Why canst not
'nounce?"

Unused to introspection he answered nothing.

" Knowst not? Shouldst know," she said
curtly. " Why dost stammer and stare ? Why
tremble? Truly 't is a blame on a man."

He had never before had the chance to look
at her so uninterruptedly and long, and made
the most of it.

" Speak, Tiber. I 'll not harm thee."

At this idea a great delighted grin crept
over his whole countenance.

" Shouldst 'nounce the Kaiser to the King,
and not budge," she declared boldly, dropping her knitting. " Seest, Tiber?" Draw

ing near, she stretched herself to an incredible height, and stood with arms akimbo, on her face an expression of delicious nonchalance. " So shouldst thou look!"

With a great mellow laugh he responded:

" I — look like thee!"

" Canst try, at least."

" Would gladly please thee, Vroni," he said simply.

She resumed her knitting. He plodded on with his protesting pen, and breathed hard with the effort.

" Tiber!"

He started.

" *Ach*, Tiber! Didst agree to stop the trembling, yet art at it soon again!"

He drooped like a remorseful dog.

" Willst learn," she remarked graciously, which instantly revived him. " I but meant to ask thee, what sort are thy people. For, take it not amiss, I once did know a little maid whom they did beat more than was meet for her, and when one but spoke on a sudden, she did tremble."

" I 've a rare good mother," he answered with profound affection. " No man hath a better."

" And thy father?"

" 'T is my stepfather, a good enough sort," he rejoined without enthusiasm, " since my mother liketh him, and he be not rough with her."

" I wager he did beat thee!" cried Vroni, pleased with her own shrewdness.

" Hardly more than his own boys — and the work had to be done," Tiber replied with philosophical objectivity.

" Seest!" she returned, and probed further. " Dost write as though thou wert ploughing a stubbly field or chopping wood. Since there be no man alive who learneth not his penning when a child, pray how, then, didst thou miss it?"

" I 'm ever slow. Thou knowst," he said meekly.

In his good eyes was some perplexity, for he was quite unused to seek connections between present effects and remote causes.

" Relate to me thy childhood," Vroni commanded, quite grave and womanly.

With somewhat broken phrases and perceptible exertion, yet with a pleasant manly ring in his voice, for the first time in his life he endeavored to give an account of himself and his deficiencies.

He had always been slow, slower than the

others. They'd all to work hard. He as the
oldest boy had to be up at three or four o'clock
in the morning to get his work done before
school, which was a good distance from the
farm. Then somehow he felt sleepy and dull
in the head, and was always falling asleep in
school, and the master had to flog him awake.
Being dull and sleepy when he got home, he
was again flogged for one thing and another
by the father. Tiber feared, with a rather
mournful smile, he had remained dull and
sleepy ever since. For sure, he had forgotten
the most the master flogged into him. At
any rate the little reading and writing he once
knew grew ever farther from him. He had
had indeed no use for learning on the farm
where he had worked till he came to serve
his time in the army.

It was the longest oration he had ever made,
but Vroni's lovely eyes were resting kindly on
him, and he found within himself as he went
on that which warmed his heart, loosed his
tongue, and revealed unhoped-for stores of
language; he only wished he might talk on
all night with that sweet maid to listen.

Again she nodded her young head and remarked oracularly: —

" Seest?   There is naught without a reason.
'T is cooking has taught me that.   How old
art thou? "

" Three and twenty."

" 'T is too old to tremble, all the same."

" Pray think not meanly of me, Vroni," he
returned quietly.   " Perchance be there man's
work to do, I fear not overmuch and waste
not time in trembling — no more it may be
than another.   'T is the 'nouncing and the
right placing of fine words that make my flesh
to creep.   Then when the gracious countess
passeth me by chance in the corridor and
turneth her head thus," he jerked his head aside
with an air of disgust as if unpleasant odors
were prevailing — " 't is then I most do shiver."

" 'T is true," Vroni observed meditatively,
" she fretted even me on the first day.   I liked
not the eyes she carried on a stick."

" I like not too well those she carrieth in her
head," rejoined Tiber, dryly.

" But gracious Comtesse Nelka?   Thou shiv-
erest not when she goes by? "

" Nay.   I 'd ride far for Comtesse Nelka."

" And I — or crawl upon my knees !   Tiber,
show me thy ink.   *Du meine Güte*, it has flies
in it ! "

"Surely not flies in winter?"

"Crumbs and black lumps that might as well be flies," she insisted, seized the inkstand, emptied, washed, and refilled it from her own bottle on a shelf. "Never again write with flies, Tiber. Hast heard?"

His happy face sought to express contrition, but could only helplessly bask in the joy of her presence.

"And mark this, Tiber: when thou dost start thy thirty-first enemies over thy paper bridge for thy ne'er-do-well Count Benno, must let them approach with two *p's*, seest? Bridge, too, for some reason or other, is penned in the schools with an *e* at its last end. Not that a letter more or less matters much. The main thing is no flies and that people know straightway what thou meanst."

"*Ach!* Hast a deal of schooling, Vroni!"

"'T is true, I 've my fair share," she admitted serenely. "I went to school till I was quite fifteen. Besides, my father knows a lot, and I take after him. 'T is for that reason I 'm not dull. Say, willst have me for thy schoolmaster instead of thy Count Benno? Then I 'll give thee a copy."

Roguish, quizzing him, yet so kind withal,

and with her brilliant beauty that bewildered him, she was attuning him to an heroic strain in which not even a copy-book could daunt him.

"Here — a fresh pen and a clean leaf."

Rather neatly, and quite boldly, from constant rapid practice in her market-book, she wrote : —

Veronika Maria Magdalena Lindl.

"Seest, Tiber, canst write me fifty Vronis, but never one with thy tongue lolling out thy mouth. Hast heard? And clutch not thy pen as if 't were saving thee from death by drowning. Make not a single smudge. Keep thy ragged letters well up on their legs, for they do fall about most piteously. Mayst also wipe thy pen once in three weeks or so, and sit up brave, and wear a pleasant countenance, and have no fit. Nay, not now, Tiber. Canst hand it to me any time within ten years."

"I 'll do it for thee, Vroni. I will remember me of every word."

"What 's thy own name?"

He told her.

"So. *Tiber Gregor Johannes Merold.* Hast that too rarely fine, and with a quirl beneath like Count Vallade's own."

A strong gleam shot over the man's face as he saw the two names, hers and his, on one page. She closed the copy-book and pushed it carelessly aside.

"Now read me something, Tiber. Will see how much of that they flogged in and out thy sleepy head."

The passage indicated at random in the newspaper, she thrust into his hands, filled him with choking wretchedness. He careered wildly through it, stopped to take breath in the middle of the long words, and gulped down the short ones whole.

"Halt, Tiber, halt! Hand me the paper. I mark but precious little sense therein."

"I, none," he groaned.

"Silver — gold — currency!" she ran her eye sagaciously over the solid column — a leader. "Ha, 't is not worth the gabble. The chief thing is to have one or the other. Either is good enough for me. But thou, Tiber, art for sure a terrible flounderer. Save the black Anastasia, I never heard thy like."

"My tongue was ever heavy."

"'T is not thy tongue alone," she retorted sharply. "'T is what lies behind. Dost not understand, Tiber. A man should under-

stand. My father understands all things."
She shook her head with serious disapproval.

"Would I were like him," Tiber said
gently, a shade of sadness in his trusty eyes.

"Fret not thyself, good Tiber," she exclaimed, with a quick, kind smile. "So that
thou standest straight, with a brave face for
all men, the learning matters little. Even I,
myself, have small concern for newspapers,
save for the market-lists, which are good reading. But 't is the butler who can tell all
the world's news, and many a time, a great
opinion."

"'T is a pretty gift," returned Tiber, with
a powerful pang of envy.

"And figures, Tiber?" she asked suddenly.
"How standest thou to thy sums?"

"Awful!" he groaned. "Hast now, Vroni,
the worst of me!"

"A man needs must be sharp at ciphering."

"Count Benno chides that I do cheat myself,
not him."

"Shouldst cheat neither thyself, nor thy
count," warned his stern pedagogue. "What
thinkst thou would become of me, could I
not reckon faster than the market wives who
seek to trip me?"

"'T is a thing, somehow, I never could beat into my pate," he said despondently.

Once more she flashed at him her warm smile of consolation.

"Never thou mind, Tiber. Art orderly, and I like thee. Yet were I thou, I 'd learn to add my columns straight. That such a man should know."

Ceaselessly in and out flew her hands. Her glance wandered fitfully around the room.

With a little laugh she remarked: —

"Dost comb thy hair straight upwards like a cock. Maybe 't is why thou sometimes lookst afraid."

"Maybe."

"A man should never be affrighted, Tiber."

"Nay, Vroni, nay. 'T is quite true. He should not."

"There be some, indeed, that make themselves too bold," she admitted, half reluctantly, and flushed slightly. "Yet," thinking of Melchior, "I like not frightened men," she added with a frown.

Tiber listened, intent and motionless.

"Men folk are little to my taste," she continued, with some asperity, "being mostly either craven things, or saucy and shiny-eyed

— except," she smiled again, and broke out radiantly, "my father. Seest, Tiber, my father has a look — not Count Vallade has the like! Nor can the young counts measure with him any day. Not Herr Eck Flemming, though he is fairly well to look upon. Not" — she hesitated, colored, and added, "not any man, though with fine clothes and friendly ways, and glad to see one when none else cares — nay, none has my father's look. None is so dear."

Tiber, leaning forward, watched her great loveliness, his dumbness struggling for expression; yet he knew too well words were not for such as he. His pale top-knot and linty eyelashes caught the light. She met his serious, manly gaze, the steadfastness of which she instinctively recognized, in spite of his peculiarities; and after a little pause, she asked kindly : —

"What thinkst thou to begin after thy time of service? Hast nearly finished, eh? Willst go back to thy mother and the farm?"

He smiled for pleasure that she spoke of his mother.

"Nay, not so soon. Am little needed there."

"Willst surely not remain in thy Count Benno's service?"

"'T is not agreed upon, but talked of many a time. He fain would keep me."

"Nay, Tiber," she protested, "take it not ill, I know 't is not my business. But if before I jested somewhat and did jeer thee, now I talk sense. Stay not too long with thy Count Benno. The life's too idle for an honest man. That much I see with my own eyes every day. Now thou art a soldier, hast enough work. But later, wert thou but his valet, thou wouldst loll too much upon thy lazy bones, and ape thy master, like the rest of them. Nay, Tiber, truly I like thee better as thou art."

"Hast reason, Vroni, and speakest sense like a man. 'T is not my wish to stay, yet one keeps sometimes what one has, rather than seek new things too long."

"'T is naught," she replied, with a peremptory wave of a knitting needle.

That quiet room, and only he and the Mädel; they two beneath one lamp; she knitting swiftly with her brown wool and big white needles, meanwhile being lovely all for him, dull, sleepy-headed Tiber; for him so

merry, kind, wise, winsome, and enchanting;
— this was more happiness than he had ever
known, almost more than he could bear.

The cuckoo clock ticked noisily. Vroni's
light click-click tapped accompaniment.
Tiber, his eyes devouring her, breathed deep.
His mental machinery moved somewhat pon-
derously, and of this fact none was so well
aware as he. But he felt he could in time
say to Vroni alone, all on his heart, the dumb,
slow thoughts, he had never expressed, —
thoughts indeed, of which he was unconscious
until she called them into being. But one
straight thing he wanted first to say, and
dared not. He had known it long, yet never
had a chance to speak, believed, too, he must
be silent always with his full heart. But
this night had brought them nearer. It was
friendly in the still room and intimate to chat
of family, home, and one's life-work. Could
he but start his heavy tongue, he'd have a
world to say to her — but of all this he had
achieved not one syllable, when suddenly
Count Benno's bell rang.

XII

FOR the unceasing festivities inevitable beneath the Vallade roof in those months,
because a charming child was about to be
devoured by an ogre, Vroni worked like a
hero. She composed exquisite dinners, and
lived up to her traditions. The more important the occasion, the more calm and masterful was she. Countess Vallade declared the
girl was worth her weight in gold, — a genius,
nothing less. Moreover, the lady, revoking
crystallized methods, issued a mandate to her
corps of domestics to presume to place no
straw of offence in Vroni's way. They one
and all might go *auf Nimmerwiedersehen*, provided she remained. She took no shade of
advantage of the augmented strength of her
position, but quietly pursued the old lines
dictated by her own sense of justice and
mother wit. Still the novel distinction left
her stranded rather higher in loneliness than

before.   Uneasy is the head that wears any
sort of crown.

During the week she desired only her work.
She rejoiced in it, and in the confidence and
respect which her ability commanded.   In
her province she perceived no drudgery.   Her
varied occupations appealed to her ambition,
her enthusiasm, her artistic sense; never
became hackneyed, but presented the rich
charm of the ever-new and unrevealed, for
she, too, like her master, "created."

But she was a young thing and ardent.   As
she became habituated to the routine of the
house, and to the group for the most part of
staid elderly servants who went their stereo-
typed way, her pleasure-loving nature ruth-
lessly demanded something more, something
which she was able to formalize only as "a
happy Sunday."   Even for such as she, it
was hardly an extravagant claim upon the
world's fund of pleasure; for what she liter-
ally meant was merely a little entertainment,
according to the simple customs of her land
and station, between the hours of four and
ten at night, every fourteen days.   She clung
obstinately to her instinct of family, and to
that broken reed Melchior, and started forth

every free day with blithest hope, as if a
miracle would intervene to silence Jakobine's
nagging. But the best that ever happened,
was that in a crowd one became sometimes
oblivious of her.

Vroni could have wept aloud with chagrin
on the afternoon she for the first time found
her brother's door aggressively locked. Incredulous, she knocked and called, but in vain.

"It is because I told Jakobine I doted on a
military band," she reflected ruefully. "Oh,
why did I say it!"

Melchior's house was one of a uniform row
of palace-servants' cottages in a paved quadrangle, with a fountain in the centre. The
houses looked deserted. All was still.

She stood irresolute. She could not bear to
turn away from that rampant inhospitality.

"Everybody is happy. Everybody is gone
somewhere. Mean, mean Jakobine!"

A brisk step crossed the quiet court.

"Well, that is bad luck!" exclaimed an
amiable voice over her shoulder. "Here let
me try," and Vincenz pounded the door
valiantly with his walking-stick.

They waited, listening, and staring in each
other's eyes.

"'T is no use," she said disconsolately. "They 've gone without me."

"Were you late?" he inquired with sympathy.

"Late!" she retorted vehemently. "I was here on the stroke of the clock. 'T is Jakobine's handiwork!"

"Jakobine should be well trounced for it."

"Oh," she returned quickly, with a frown, "speak rather of what concerns you."

"Vincenz, my boy, go slow!" he said to himself.

"I understood you to remark — "

She checked him, not without dignity: —

"That is quite different. Even if my tongue be quick, a stranger need not notice it. Jakobine is my brother's wife — hateful though she be, and hard of heart on this fine Sunday! But what is that to you? Why do you linger here?"

He laughed pleasantly.

"Come, I like that. I happened to be passing. I have friends living — over there," with a conveniently large gesture. "I stopped an instant to see if I could help you. It seemed a shame, a young maid should be left all alone, and the door locked flat against her."

Vroni drew a long breath, and squeezing back two tears, smouldered like a grieved child.

"And 't is the Grenadier Band!" she sighed. She stood on the door-stone, a little above him, was arrayed in her best, which was neat, dark, and plain, not without distinct refinement. The man watched her eagerly.

"And what, if I may ask, are you going to do now?"

"Nothing," she replied mournfully. "Nothing at all."

"I think that is quite too bad."

She nodded in sad acquiescence, and pitied herself vastly.

"'T is bad, indeed."

"Now what if you and I should take a little quiet walk together?" he suggested, in a friendly and matter-of-fact tone.

"I did think of that myself," she returned seriously; "but then you see we do not know each other, and my father would not think it seemly."

"Ah — you have known me months and months."

"In a round-the-corner sort of way. 'T is no straight acquaintanceship."

"Ah — after all the shoe-leather I've worn out in following you."

"'T was your own foolishtry," she retorted stoutly. "Nobody asked you."

"Answer me this. Have I been patient? Have I respected your wish? Have I obeyed your least word?"

"'T is true."

They had strolled slowly half across the quadrangle, and stood involuntarily by the fountain.

"If I knew what to do with myself," he remarked, with amiable ingenuousness. "I am quite alone, too. It is odd enough, but my friends also have left me in the lurch."

"'T is a great shame," she cried warmly.

"Yes, is n't it? So I merely thought, both being in the same boat, it would be reasonable to take a little outing together."

"Truly, it sounds reasonable," sighed Vroni.

"Particularly as I am acquainted with your brother."

"Oh, are you?" she smiled, radiant.

"And it seemed to me we might look him up — follow after, don't you know? Suppose we should just go up to the Hunter's Horn

to hear the Grenadier Band, and find him?
What could be more simple than that?"

She clasped her hands in delight.

"And surprise Frau Jakobine," he suggested farther.

"*Sapristi!* 'T would but serve her right."

Why not, instead of going home to bewail
her lot, do what would be really clever and
desirable, what, in fact, might be called her
plain duty, — assert, for once, her independence, and enjoy herself to the top of her
bent, in despite of Jakobine. Vroni regarded
the man's friendly face. He sat on the low
moulding of the fountain, tapped his boot
with his cane, and kept his alert eyes fixed on
hers.

"I don't know what I'm waiting for," she
said slowly. For still something seemed
distinctly to restrain her word of assent, and
bid her to forego this step.

He got up.

"I'll not urge you. Why should you go
unwillingly. 'T was not to trouble you that
I spoke. I will go to the Horn myself, for
the music will be great. If I spy your
brother and his wife, I'll say I left you here.
So good-by, and a pleasant evening to you."

He took off his hat, and turned away slowly.

Vroni saw the staring row of little empty houses; she saw the broad blue sky, and felt the fresh air on her cheek.

"Wait," she cried, "I 'll just go along a bit."

Out of the town and up a long hill, the two walked together. It was the last of February, and spring coming on apace. Vroni laughed, glowed, and sparkled. Vincenz was careful to tell her only innocuous tales of his wide wanderings, such as he deemed would not alarm or vex her, for he had wit enough to perceive she was not as many he had known and knew. They spoke, too, of themselves, how persistently he had haunted her path. Once he had darted from behind a statue of a mounted king, and startled her. They laughed at the remembrance. Then the day he stood at the flower booth. Then that day in the rain. And when a nursery-maid upset her perambulator, and the morning the dragoons rode past. Already a host of droll and familiar reminiscences.

In the large, brilliantly-lighted pavilion on the hill, she sat in a corner, slowly sipped her beer, and looked blissfully about upon hundreds of couples, — husbands and wives, brothers and sisters, sweethearts, at many tables, children too. Nobody minded her and Berg. She wondered she had hesitated an instant, it was all so simple and delightful. The tone was gently gay; faces were kind, voices happy. This was what she had craved. It was life. Her eyes grew starry; her cheeks and lips glowed like rich flowers; she gave Vincenz friendly and grateful glances.

"'T is strange, I spy not my Melchior and his Jakobine."

"'T is strange, indeed," agreed the man, who had seen them making for quite a different quarter.

"Would they could see me now! Would they'd walk in!"

Vincenz made a queer grimace.

"I wish that less."

"Why?"

"Well — I'd rather have you all to myself."

She gave him a shrewd glance.

"Hm! I believe you know my brother not at all."

"I may not know him very well. I met him once in a crowd of men, you see. Probably he has forgotten me."

"Doubtless," she returned dryly, adding, after a few moments, gravely: "'T is a poor thing to tell fibs. As for me, I cannot stomach them. Mind that if you want more than a round-the-corner acquaintanceship with me."

"Never fear. 'T is my habit to speak by the book. ' A man, — a word,' say I."

"How beautiful 't is here," she exulted, "and how they 'll be astonished!"

"Do you think you 'd better tell them?" he asked quite tranquilly.

She looked apprehensively at him.

"Perhaps I 'll not tell them just yet, for I do fear me Jakobine would never let me come again."

"Confound Jakobine!" he remarked heartily, and Vroni smiled.

While she sat thrilling and throbbing with the music, which now strangely softened her bright face as with a veil of tender and half regretful memories, now swept her soul toward unimagined realms of recklessness, far away on the Rough Alp in the little cottage by the crag, Dionysius the weaver lay dying, his last thought, unutterable love for his Mädel.

His children, or most of them at least,

gathered at the homestead for the funeral, —
Vroni frantic with sorrow. But something
strange was sent to steady her, and give her
strength to endure. Agathe's great strength
and rude health succumbed like a blasted oak.
Helpless and gentle, she lay ill; and, the
others leaving, except Sebastian, who stayed
to regulate affairs, Vroni tended her. In a
couple of weeks she, too, passed away. All
that she said of the weaver was — her meek,
bewildered eyes gazing at his loom — the oft-
repeated, apologetic murmur: —

"Seest, Vroni, I was used to him."

"Truly, mother," the heartbroken girl
would answer, as if soothing a child, "wast
used to him."

So Agathe died, of a cold and strain the
neighbors said; and Sebastian gave his half-
stunned little sister much excellent advice,
and returned to his vegetables and devotions.
She, with her poignant heart-ache for the
weaver, and most pitiful in her remembrance
of the tempestuous mother, so softened in
those last days, took with her some recently
spun rolls of fine linen, marked *For Vroni*, and
promptly resumed her duties in the Vallade
house. Simple folk waste little time upon

the luxury of prolonged and visible mourning. Work they have always with them.

In her vast homesickness and longing, as she came from ineffectual attempts at intercourse with Melchior and Jakobine back to the stately house where none cared for herself, but only for her skilled productions; where no older and more experienced woman sought to discover her human needs, to comfort and sustain her young, sad heart; where Comtesse Nelka, it is true, murmured a few gentle, pitying words to her upon her return, but never again, after that first delightful essay, was permitted to find time to cheer herself and a sister-girl with kind companionship and sympathy, — Vincenz Berg never lost an opportunity to meet her, was always near at hand, friendly, and solicitous.

In her extravagant moods he suited her well. At other times she would turn upon him with sudden, undefined mistrust; for he had ways and words that jarred upon her when he was off his guard. For her deeper feelings, the strength of her affection for her dead father and her mountain home, she perceived instinctively Vincenz had no comprehension; and after one or two attempts, when she looked at him strangely as if across a chasm, she banished him completely from that sanctuary.

But he offered certain compensations for his hollowness and flippancy. He was adroit, experienced, and full of worldly tact. He made things kindly for her when the world was gloomy. He comforted her at first, with his devoted presence, and, as time went on, cheered her with sunny and amiable nonsense. Being in love with her, he appeared at his best, and at his worst was no monster of iniquity, but merely a careless young fellow — of the baser sort. He made love to her with gentleness, not too precipitately, and she was young, and alone but for him.

Fearing Jakobine's interference, Vroni met him clandestinely. She gradually ceased her regular visits at Melchior's, and her eagerness to go about with them cooled visibly. Jakobine's lovelessness palled in truth upon the young girl, after Vincenz's soft and unfailing devotion.

On a certain Sunday, Jakobine sent her a message, bidding her not to call for them as agreed, for they were invited by old friends. Vroni, in the singularly effervescent mood

into which recovery from the weaver's be-
queathed headache was apt to plunge her, — a
mood of physical languor and gayest irrespon-
sibility, — started out with Vincenz.

It was June weather. In the perfumed
breath of earth, of fields and woods, where
they strayed, in the scent of myriad roses,
laburnum, and acacia drooping rich with sweetness over high garden walls, in the love-
glances, song, and happy laughter of scores of
youths and maids, merry in groups, or steal-
ing off by twos to whisper together in the
twilight, was a vast and subtle intoxication.
That day they wandered far.

While those below the salt were thus enact-
ing their humble destinies, Eck Flemming
had long since sailed away, as secretary to his
scientific and exploring expedition; Nelka
von Vallade was engaged to be married to
Baron Frege; and for their lives neither of
the two could have told how it all came about.

Nothing whatever of an agitated nature
transpired, not even a little wee promise of
eternal fidelity. Countess Vallade took good
care to prevent solecisms. The atmosphere
was balmy to the last, when "dear Eck was

so unexpectedly whisked away." His party, after long preliminaries, had, it seemed, suddenly determined to set off at an earlier date than that appointed, and Eck was summoned by telegraph to join his chief at Marseilles.

Dearest Nelka happened to be staying a couple of days with friends in the country, when dear Eck came to make his hurried farewells. He had most unfortunately but a few hours in town, for his young orphan sisters were naturally entitled to his last moments. Besides, the business arrangements dear Eck so nobly made for them demanded some little time. Eck was a noble fellow, and nobility of sentiment and deed always, the countess stated as her firm belief, carried within itself its sure reward. Dearest Nelka would be quite inconsolable, for Eck was as dear to her as her brothers.

The count embraced him affectionately but with a *distrait* air, and, waiving acknowledgments of influence and protection, told him his future was now assured.

"With your ability and energy — don't speak of it, my dear boy, not worth mentioning — a brilliant career, and one after your own heart. Ah, my dear boy, if I were

young again and in your shoes! Africa is
the place for a man to-day."

He then rang a bell, gave some papers and
orders to the man who answered it, fum-
bled with a pile of documents, ran his hand
brusquely through his hair, and, with a somewhat wandering eye, added : —

"I congratulate you, my dear boy, I congratulate you, upon my word."

Although the moment seemed but too plainly
to invite a prompt exit rather than confi-
dences, Flemming had, he believed, no choice
but to avail himself as best he might of its
unpropitiousness. As he opened his mouth
to ask the very fidgety gentleman for his
daughter, in clanked Benno, — "Arm'd, say
you? Arm'd, my lord!" — from the expression of whose face as well as his father's,
presumably by appointment. Benno drawled
Africa was "*pyramidal;*" Eck "*colossal*
lucky*" and a "*phenomenal* good fellow"; —
and love's young dream was crowded out.

Flemming went to his hotel, and wrote a
letter to Comtesse Nelka. It was long, warm,
straightforward, manly, and resolute. It displayed, although a love-letter, and written
in desperate haste by a soldier of fortune, a

praiseworthy degree of common sense; like the heart which inspired it, was torn and baffled by the grief of so inadequate parting, yet rang with a brave strain of comfort and protection that would have endued Nelka with joyous strength to wait and hope. In short, it was a very good letter, but it went astray, — letters, like emotions, sometimes do even in the best of families.

Had Nelka been opposed or provoked to demonstration, she might have discovered her latent power. But everybody was devoted to her; she was petted, caressed, adored. Her three brothers could hardly have been more tender to a lady-love. Many nights for many weeks she wept herself to sleep because Eck had gone off without a word, and she thought of him continually as was her habit for years. They had always cared for each other; that was a matter of course, and they had said it, too, in words. But it grew with time more and more evident that what her mother called "the immeasurable ambition of youth" had drifted him away from his little friend and sweetheart.

Every one spoke of him with frank affection. None sought to spare her feelings, or

seemed, indeed, to assume that she had any
sensitiveness concerning him. She fell in
with their method, and gave no sign, except
that she was a little listless. They prophe-
sied great things of him. Clotilde, who had
returned from extensive travels, stated with
conviction that Eck would never marry, at
least not for years, for he was too clever not
to realize a wife would be but an impediment
in the high flight he contemplated.

Nelka rather liked the splendid stones
flashing upon her hand, but grew silent and
apathetic in the presence of her elderly lover.
Still, she was hurried so adroitly from one
thing to another, she really had little time to
be consciously miserable.

Count Waldemar, her favorite brother,
whom she saw infrequently, he being stationed at a distant garrison, looked rather
gravely at her when he first saw her after the
engagement.

"Well, lambkin," he said, "what's all
this? Rough on you, eh?"

"I don't mind much," she replied list-
lessly, which was true at the moment, for
Baron Frege was not near. "See, Waldemar,
this is the ring. This tiny butterfly watch

came yesterday. Something or other comes every day."

He put his arm round her.

"Nelka dear, never mind those things. I do not understand — "

"What don't you understand, dear Waldemar? Nelka, my darling, you must hurry a little, or you will be late to dinner. Now, Waldemar?"

"I don't like it," he said bluntly. "It's abominable, you know!"

"You see for yourself she is happy."

"She is a baby. She has no conception what the fellow is. I don't like it, nor does Knod. We cannot get our bearings. Was there no trouble when Eck left?"

"None, whatever," replied the countess, blandly.

"It is deuced queer. I'm awfully sorry I did not see him at the last. I did my best, but could not get off in time — I could have sworn — "

"Well?"

"It is no use," he broke out. "You know we lieutenants don't believe in much, but we believe in love," and restlessly paced the room.

"My dear Waldemar," returned the countess, cool and clear. "Permit me to inquire upon what Nelka and Eck Flemming would have lived? Besides, so far as I know, he said nothing explicit to her. Would you have me fling her at him?"

He stared at her questioningly.

"I think you men frequently make radical mistakes in your premises. Love, in its legitimate place, of course, is an excellent thing; but not all women feel as intensely as you may imagine. Not every girl is a potential volcano. Nelka has a sweet, affectionate, malleable disposition, — not at all sensational. In our family, on either side, I may say, we have never, happily, produced Brunhildas. I do not doubt she will be very happy and content."

"With that old rake!"

"A man of the world, a man, I concede, of large experience — but leading at present a most exemplary life."

"The devil he does," muttered Waldemar.

"Then freshness and innocence have a marvellous influence."

"Swindle," he murmured, shaking his head.

"At all events," she added, in a tone that

meant business, "may I beg *you* not to interfere? You see for yourself, Nelka is in brilliant health and spirits. Ah, if you lieutenants
who believe in love," tapping him playfully
on the cheek, "were a little less self-indulgent,
and made less heavy demands upon your families! The sad truth is, no young men need
an inexhaustibly rich brother-in-law more
than you, Benno, and Knod. Particularly
Benno. But I suppose you, too, have not
come home without a purpose, eh? Well,
then, don't interfere. The beautiful sister
of three young men living at your pace, can
hardly enact an African idyl. What if she
also were always draining your poor father?
Do you happen to know what her absolutely
indispensable toilettes cost a year? No, no.
Some things are preposterous from the start.
All is for the best, and I am thankful matters
have gone off so pleasantly."

"I cannot help it, it's a beastly shame,"
muttered Waldemar, gnawing his moustache;
but he did not interfere, and when certain
revelations, and a strong appeal, reached him
from Africa, it was, indeed, too late.

XIII

IT was, Countess Vallade declared, a *bouleversement* as disastrous as unapprehended, and, just before the wedding, annoying beyond expression. Could Nelka but have been persuaded to consent to an earlier day than the seventh of December; but in that one respect she had been inexorable. When they urged her, she emerged from her gentle passivity and became actually wild, even threatening to run away and hide herself. Clotilde, whose judgment and influence upon her sister had been most invaluable, advised temporizing still. Clotilde suspected Nelka might be waiting for something, — a day, an anniversary perhaps, and what it might bring. Clotilde dimly recalled some fancy of the sort in her own sentimental days. Whatever it brought was laid with similar objects, — unopened of course; there were some things a wellbred woman never could stoop to do, — and tied with a blue ribbon in the countess's secret drawer.

So month after month they had humored the child, — inconvenient, in fact precarious as the situation was, and now in this most inopportune moment Countess Vallade had to discharge Vroni forthwith. Not only in the interests of respectability and morality must she go, but also on account of dearest Nelka, who had a curious weakness for the girl. Nelka was in an unaccountable mood as her wedding day approached. She must not be farther excited or disturbed. She ought not to be informed of the deplorable circumstance. Vroni was perfection in her department. The countess even contemplated re-engaging her later, — provided she reformed and became steady; but for the present one had unfortunately no choice. Decency demanded the sacrifice, and dearest Nelka must be screened.

But on the evening Vroni was to leave the house, Comtesse Nelka, in ivory white silk and on her fair throat five rows of pearls, the gift of Baron Frege, rushed into the kitchen and after her a startled valet with a great white-fur-lined cape.

"Where is she? I will see her!" she said peremptorily, and Vroni came.

"I always liked you, you know, Vroni," exclaimed the comtesse excitedly, stretching out her bare white arms, " and I always shall."

The two girls looked an instant straight in each other's eyes. One face was no paler than the other. Nelka gave a little sob. At this Vroni shivered, seized the extended hands, and kissed them many times with quick hot kisses, but spoke no word.

Next to Tiber, she had dreaded seeing Nelka. Vroni thought she could face all the world better than Tiber's honest eyes. It was long before she saw them again.

"You should not take it so to heart, dear child," the countess said late that night to Nelka, sobbing in her bed. "You may believe me when I assure you the lower classes have not our power of keen suffering. Less sensitively organized, they do not feel as we do. I 've seen them bury their children, shed no tear, and go to work. It is terribly shocking, Vroni's case, and heartless enough, just after her parents' death. You see it is as I say, they are destitute of feeling. Don't cry so, dear."

But Nelka sobbed on inconsolable — for whom, for what, and whether all for Vroni, she did not say.

Jakobine was in no respect surprised. Had she not from the first perceived Vroni's utter want of principle? In fact, the woman's satisfaction in having her prognostications so incontrovertibly justified seemed somewhat greater than even her condemnation of the culprit.

Melchior was cut to the heart, — wounded in his sham respectability as well as in his honest family pride, and in his affections; for, in his feeble way, he was fond of his young sister. His affection, it is true, possessed the stamina of limp whalebone, and invariably collapsed when needed; still it was a species of human attachment, and it suffered because of Vroni's mischance.

He had an interview with Vincenz, and, Jakobine not being present, said what he ought, and appeared very like a man. Berg, all in all, made no bad impression. He expressed undying affection for Vroni, and the firm intention of marrying her the first moment circumstances, the obstructive force of which he more or less vaguely explained, would permit. It seemed to Melchior, after he had partially recovered from his first shock, that if his club associates should hear nothing of it, and happily not every one knew he had a sister, and if Sebastian and Sister Corona were not informed, at all events, not immediately, for they would certainly hold him responsible, the matter, bad as it was, might be patched and smoothed over. Though Berg hinted at temporary embarrassment, he was a high-class workman and earned handsomely. After some years nobody would suspect there had been the slightest irregularity. Melchior had attained to these more mellow views when he went to see Vroni in the room she had rented upon leaving the Vallades.

"Take a chair, brother," she said, sat down herself, and watched him.

"I never expected to see this day," he began laboriously.

"Now, Melchior," she returned, her tone hard and quiet, "I know all thou wouldst say, and have no mind to hear it. Suppose thou holdest thy peace."

He hesitated before whimpering : —

"I had not hoped to find thee unrepentant, Vroni."

"Am no sort that howls in full church to waken pity!" she retorted defiantly.

"Jakobine says—"

" That least of all things will I hear, not being of an over-patient nature."

Once or twice he tried to speak.

She interrupted : —

" Canst tell me naught. Canst change naught. Waste not thy words. Leave me to go my way."

He rose at length and looked at her helplessly, such affection as he had working in his face.

" I feel like death about thee, Vroni," he said quite simply. " Wast such a merry little maid at home."

She turned pale.

" And father — "

She left him standing, ran swiftly into the next room, and locked the door.

Vroni had been fortunate enough to find lodgings with a kindly woman, and occasional work at a pastry-cook's in the vicinity. Her evenings were spent usually at some place of amusement with Vincenz. She seemed utterly reckless, and greedy for excitement. The society of coarse and boisterous men and women, and loud gay music that drowned reminiscence, best suited her mood; for only amid rollicking noise and mad laughter could

she for brief intervals cease to see the pale
stern face of Dionysius the weaver, always
turned away, never the smile of content, and
the beautiful eyes looking down in love upon
her, as when she used to walk hand in hand
with him through the cornfields. *Ach Gott!*
Were she but back again a little child in the
old days; wild, naughty, and rebellious, to be
regarded severely, sent supperless to bed,
chastised with the big pewter spoon, but forgiven at last and loved again. Because she
could not bear such thoughts, or the weaver's
averted face, she plunged deeper into the
mire.

Long before her child was born she had
fathomed Vincenz's shallowness and insin-
cerity. This was her worst punishment. Yet
being affectionate, and used to him and his
pleasant plausible ways, — looking forward too
to a whole long life with him, she made the
best of him, as women will, and sought to
believe in him even when she knew him to be
smoothly deceiving her, — thereby becoming
herself less honest in her effort to live down
to his level.

More than a year had passed and still they
were not married. Vincenz's reasons varied

with the amount of liquor he drank, which was sometimes excessive; yet in no mood, however unstable in other respects, was he otherwise than amiable and devoted to her. Her baby daughter she was fond of, but not immeasurably. She tended it without rapture, wistfully, finding in it no joy or consolation. Maternal love dawns slowly in some hearts, popular belief to the contrary notwithstanding.

It was a strange and miserable time. Vincenz was sinking lower and lower in her estimation — she herself, alas, also. Sometimes she longed to cut those wretched years of degradation out of her life, as one amputates a diseased limb, and cleanse herself in healing waters. But for the most part she but lived on day by day, appearing in no respect to quarrel with her destiny. Whatever her private meditations, no face was gayer than hers at the jovial suppers they frequented, no tongue more ready and droll. They went often to theatres too, and heard much music, which both loved.

Yet more and more she was withdrawing into an inner life remote from Vincenz. Of her finer self he had no appreciation, and she

long since had ceased to reveal it to him. Of
her father she never spoke; but night and day
his face, still unreconciled, pursued her. She
would plead with him by the hour, entreat,
explain piteously how, step by step, it had all
come about, beg him to see how she, at heart,
loathed her life. Not once had he relented.
Melchior she saw no more, except in the distance, towering most English on the box.
Once she sprang quickly into a shop to avoid
meeting Tiber, striding along in a postman's
uniform, his tow-head well up, his face placid
and dutiful.

Little Anita she now sent to the care of her
sister Marie and Tante Ursula, since a second
child was imminent. Vincenz, after frequent
and too copiously explained absences, had at
last taken the necessary steps toward marriage.
Vroni, silent, listless, in a strangely bitter
mood, listened one evening to his complacent
flippant talk of the banns published at the
Rathhaus, and of the civil and religious ceremonies to take place in four days.

"For the child's sake, I fain would have it —
since 't is better for it to be born in wedlock,"
was her singular remark.

"For naught else, Vroni?" he demanded

with the complacent air of one who knows the
worth of what he bestows.

" Nay, I know not."

" Wouldst tease me," he said with a smile.

She shook her head gravely, and after some
moments said : —

" Knowst I did never question thee or seek
to hurry thy plans."

"True, Vroni. There was never one like
thee for not pestering a man."

" Seest, Vincenz, my Nita has no father.
Nor will my poor baby soon to come have
but a scrap of one to cover it — since the blessing of holy Church but barely falls before its
birth. I would ask thee now, since we twain
are to be man and wife, why hast thou de-
layed so long? What need hadst thou to do
my little ones a wrong? This is of late my
thought."

" Why, Vroni, puttest things strangely, upon
my word. *Thy* little ones! And since all
will so soon be well, why so solemn-eyed?
I scarce see in thee to-night my lightsome
maid."

" I would know, Vincenz."

" Have I not told thee oft enough? I was
but waiting to take proper rooms and live as

would befit thee. Besides I have had certain
large demands to meet, through no fault of
my own, except that my name was on a friend's
note. Such things do oft arrive to vex a
man."

"Truly it seems most strange," she said
slowly, "since I do earn well, and gladly would
have helped thee."

"*Ach*, Vroni, let us not be gloomy; I meant
no harm, and do love thee beyond reason."

"Willst not speak out fair to me, Vincenz?
Trust me, and I 'll stand by thee; but I breathe
ill where lies are in the air," and she brushed
her hand with a curious gesture across her face,
as if cobwebs were clinging there.

"Hast a queer mood on thee, but 't will
pass," Vincenz rejoined indulgently, and chatted
of the wedding supper, to which many guests
were bidden. Melchior had promised to honor
the occasion with his presence, and even Jakobine was deliberating. After all a wedding,
any wedding, was respectable.

The next morning, Vroni received an anonymous letter.

"Surely thou believest not such an inven-
tion?" he cried, blustering, as she showed it
him.

"God knows I would fain believe thee for my children's sake "

" Anonymous letters always lie."

" Mayhap, for 't is a false way to strike one down."

"'T is some fool jealous of thy pretty looks and minded to make mischief," he protested with a laugh.

She regarded him in silence with intelligent eyes. She detected the false note in his voice. Suddenly she said : —

" Vincenz, I pray thee, tell me the truth — this once."

" I 've naught to tell thee," he returned sulkily.

" Trust me, Vincenz," she pleaded.

" Come now, 't is unlike thee, this suspicion, this jealousy."

" I am not jealous. I want but truth between us. Seest, Vincenz, I will forgive thee whatever it may be, so thou be but an honest man and speakest truth."

Vincenz had fully recovered his self-possession.

" Hast naught to forgive, my dear, except it be I am a fool about thee."

Brushing her face with the palms of both hands, she cried passionately : —

"Thou makst it so that I cannot breathe!
Knowst me so little after all this time? How
can I live with thee in falsehood? We twain
stand almost before God's altar. Vincenz, I
pray thee, for my children's sake, give me
true speech."

"Nay, Vroni, calm thyself. Hast never yet
made me such a scene," he responded coax-
ing and laughing a little. "Willst marry me
fast enough" — his glance resting significantly
upon her — "I have no fear. Why makst so
big strange eyes? But it matters not. I
know thou 'rt not well. — Show me thy frock."

On her bed lay her wedding-dress, the customary black cashmere of girls of her station.
Vincenz took from a box he had brought a
wreath of waxen myrtle blossoms for her hair
and a spray for the throat.

"Seest? Now shouldst smile a bit on me.
Ach was!" he exclaimed lightly in response to
her look of pain. "That's nothing. Everybody wears it."

"If I must deck myself, I will wear violets,"
she answered low, and remembered those few
precious ones she used to find beneath the
hedge and show with jubilant cries to the
weaver at his loom.

"Old women wear violets," laughed Vincenz. ".Art but a young thing, Vroni — and pretty art thou beyond all I've seen, so that a man has no choice but to love thee."

"Dost love me for naught else but my looks?" she asked, her gaze fixed upon the myrtle wreath in her hand.

"Surely such looks as thine are the best reason in the world to love a woman," he replied, and kissed her heartily.

" He would have me wear myrtle before the altar," she was thinking with sickening disgust. "'T is what he is.   Myrtle!"

She stood at her window and watched him saunter away with a dandy step and whistling a lively street tune. He did not suspect her suffering. Whenever she turned to him with any message from within, they were as far apart as two strangers passing each other without a glance. They did not belong together, never had belonged together. It was not only that his words were lies. He himself was a lie — a pleasant, laughing, wily, hollow lie.

While she stood still holding in her hands the waxen mockery, a woman, breathless, distraught, — threatening, indeed until she apprehended her rival's hopeless mood, came in

and laid bare Vincenz's life, her own and
other lives, all wretched through his baseness,
all clamoring for redress and claiming him.

The woman, who had a pretty though haggard face, was perhaps four or five and twenty,
Vroni saw, and a peasant like herself.

She heard the whole tale with no word of
interruption.   In many points it resembled
her own experience.

"Why comst so late?" she asked at length
with white stiff lips.

The girl sobbed : —

"I heard not long ago, but he told me
't was not true.   He had no thought of marriage with thee."

"Truly, 't was like him," Vroni said, deadly
pale but quiet save for her blazing eyes.

"And he gave me the money for our passage out, and said he would follow in the next
weeks, so soon as he could close up his affairs.
But I, for some slight reason and only at the
last, — I trusted not his speech."

"Wait.   Let me think.   Didst write me this
letter?"

"Nay.   I wrote it not."

"'T is well for thy tale.   I were loath to believe one who stabs in the dark."

" Canst believe me," said the girl, simply.

"I believe thee.   Hast an honest way with thee though thou be a fool like me.   Mayhap after all the writer of the letter is another. Truly a tidy wedding company."

The girl sobbed on.

" How many children hast thou?"

" Three."

" Thy youngest — of what age?"

The girl told her.   It was rather younger than her Nita.   Vroni covered her face with her hand and sat rigid for some moments, her soul staggering.

"Art thou poor?" she asked at length, abruptly.

" Ah, yes, that I am.   'T is little he can bring me, and I am not well, being worn and weary."

" Thou sayest thou dost trust no smile, no word, no good deed of his?"

" Nay, I trust, forgetting; but never when I am in fair sense and do remember."

" Dost like him?"

" Did he take me out and make much of me as once he used, yes, surely I do like him fairly well.   Hath a pleasant way with him, when he's not angered."

"And dost want him still; wouldst take him?" demanded Vroni, in her voice an icy contempt — for the woman, for herself, for them all, for the ghastliness of life.

"Surely, since he alone can give me back my good name."

"*Ach Gott!*" exclaimed Vroni, and laughed low in ineffable dreariness.

The woman looked wonderingly at her.

"Go now," said Vroni, with deadly quiet; "I think I can bear thee here no more. Canst have the man. Mayst do what thou willst with him without fear of me. Here, take this," thrusting the wedding dress into the astonished woman's arms, "and this," giving her the myrtle, "and this, and this. Nay, thank me not. 'T is thine most willingly. Am sorry for thee," she said more gently. "Truly I never meant to rob thee. But go now, for 't is not in my nature to bear more."

After some hours of dry-eyed still misery, she dragged herself into a church and knelt, shuddering, behind a pillar.

"Father," she prayed, not to Him in heaven or to any interceding saint, but straight from her tortured heart to Dionysius the weaver, "seest, here will I stay till thou dost speak to me, till thou dost help. Hast not punished me long enough? 'T is more than two years now since thou hast looked on me. Yet didst use to love me well!

"Gaze not aside and far above me, turn kind eyes on me and forgive. Have pity on thy Mädel! Seest, father, am a rarely wicked maid; have been so without head or care or thought, so mad-like, yet never did I truly mean to be bad. Must know that well, thyself, father. Art so wise."

Behind her sheltering pillar she crouched lower, huddled in her shawl. The church was fragrant, dim, and still. Now and again crisp footsteps echoed along the stone floor. She heard nothing but the cry of her own heart.

"Seest, father, there is my Nita and this my other child. *So ist's.* Were Vincenz an honest man, I would forgive. Could forgive his lightness and his feather-talk when my heart is heavy as lead, could forgive the drink, the cards, and the women; should mind the women, but could bear it and forgive and be a trusty wife to him were his thought straight and clean, and his tongue brave. Seest thyself, father, 't is most plain, I and my children cannot house with lies.

That thou couldst never abide. For such
good name as such a man can give, I care
naught. Can he then give me that which he
hath not? Shall his poor name shrive me for
my sin? Nay, 't were not sense or right —
't were a most monstrous lie.

"Didst use once to press thy good hands on
my head. Ah, it has ached so and had such
evil thoughts since thou didst die and leave thy
little maid alone. Canst hold out so rarely
long against me? Thee I would forgive for
aught that thou couldst do. Once couldst
look stern for a while, yet afterwards didst
ever comfort me. Comfort me now, my
father. Sore am I driven — helpless, broken,
and know not whither to go.

"'T was from the very first he lied to me;
but I was careless, and light of head, and
comprehended not. Never an hour since I
knew him but he has deceived me. All that
seemed pleasantness was foul. And the other
girl and her poor children, and other women
and theirs, he, all smiles and lies for many
women, yet caring naught! 'T is shame to
be a man, and wound hearts so! And bitter
shame is on me and thee and thy good name.
Yet did I drown myself, Nita might miss for

somewhat I could give. 'T is this that is the
end of my thought, howe'er I do turn it long
hours in my mind.

"Dost mind thee of that witch-night long
ago, when I was small, and great winds shook
the cottage till all upon the shelves did
quake? Most gently did the mother cheer
Brindle, and bid her be of a stout heart,
and after did stand and speak her mind, 'and
make a giant shadow on the wall. And gruff
Bastian did fume and rage at thee. Wast
mending thy shuttle, and stooping o'er it in
thy hands. Then didst raise thy head, and
say there be steep paths and no hand near.
' Poor lad, poor lad,' didst say full soft, and
wast sorry for him with thine eyes. Thou,
father, 't is thy Vroni on the jagged path, and
knows not which way to turn. 'T is her heart
that 's faint, 't is her head that 's wild. Willst
not yet say poor maid? nor lay thine hand
upon the aching head? Willst ever turn
away?

"Yet art listening. Dost but make as
though thou heardst not. 'T is to try me, I
know full well. Yet I pray thee in thy
mercy, not over long now in this hour, — not
beyond thy child's last strength which is so

spent, though heavy chastisement do I deserve.
Hearken while I do tell thee all.

"My Nita I was loving not enough at first.
I mind me I was frozen-like. Now I love
every hair on her soft head. Yet this child
more, — this most, — for this one is my
sin.

"Save God above, and His great saints and
angels, so far far off from such as me, thou,
father, thou alone dost hear, shallst read my
heart. Did no folk know, I'd scarce to shame
myself for Nita. Seest, I was so heedless
and so young. I'll not, indeed, make mean
excuse. Yet truly I did seek and foresee no
harm at all, and had no evil thought, save
giddily to run about for music, mirth, and
good cheer.

"But for this, my poor, poor child, I do
shame myself, before my very self, and not
before men who are now naught to me. For
I had learned to know what Vincenz was,
though I did shut my eyes and make as
though I saw not. In my most inner thought
I did know and understand, yet lived on in
the mire being once therein. And because
this child is shame and sin, I do love it with
a pity high as heaven for the wrong that I do

give it with its life. Through this child,
too, I love my Nita better. This child, my
sin, is waking me to love that none may
measure save thou that once didst love me
so. Truly, this child doth teach me wider
thought.

"Here do I lie till thou dost take me back.
I cannot live without thee. Have grown
worse and worse since thou hast ceased to
smile. Help thy poor Mädel. Be good to
me. Love me again. Seest not, it but makes
me bad when thou art stern so long? Ah,
we do need thee, I and my Nita and this, my
sad heart's child! For their sakes forgive.
Wast ever fair and straight in thy ways.
Thinkst thou to punish them for their mother's
fault? Then for once hast not right and reason on thy side, and that I tell thee to thy
face! Ah! come to us. Ah! leave us not.
Show me the way my weary feet must tread.
Abide with me and mine that I may find
strength to go on, and never grieve thee more.
Vater, lieb Väterchen!"

It was the blind organist's hour.

He sat in his accustomed place, and his
soul spoke.

His loneliness, his sorrow welled forth, and

filled the silence of the lofty vaults. His
slow plaint trembled on the incense-laden air,
hovered over the few isolated penitents, and
compassed the prostrate woman round about
with the sweet marvel of its lamentation.

She ceased to shudder and to sob. She lay
quite still, and waited.

The blind musician questioned, rebelled,
and stormed. At the very foot of the altar
surged and crashed his sea of tumult, and
broke in slow innumerable sobbing.

Vroni lay motionless as death.

Above the mighty moving flood of tone, a
voice began, calm, divine, compassionate. It
ceased and spoke again. It responded pitifully to the many sobbing strains. Sighing,
one by one died away their moans, dominated
by the inexorable insistence of its peace,— the
sacred and inscrutable peace of the human
soul that through agony has learned its
lesson of submission. And amid victorious
heavenly harmonies, Vroni at last felt the
loved hand, so long withdrawn, pressed on
her throbbing head. Again the weaver stood
with her and searched her face with the old
gentle questioning and no more sternness in
the dear brown eyes.

The blind man played on. Vroni knelt long. Into her thought came light and unity. She saw her way, her immediate way, stretching stern before her, and undismayed set off upon its thorns.

XIV

WHEN young Vroni was dancing innocently along the short cut to perdition, no hand was stretched out to restrain her, no voice warned. While she lived a loose, demoralizing life in quasi-marriage, and an environment of more or less ribald companions and tawdry pleasures, her intimate censors were less shocked than they pretended, and left her to her own devices. The avowed intention of the young couple to commit matrimony sooner or later lent a species of domestic halo to their irregular relationship, and in point of social morals distinguished them indeed from the majority of their motley associates.

But when, with a strong spiritual revolt, she shook off childishness, bewilderment, and inertia, rose from the slime into which she had fallen, consciously willed to return to the old cleanliness, and bravely assumed the burden, for life, of the two luckless little memo-

rials of their parents' selfishness, vast and
fierce was the storm of condemnation she
evoked, and all her little world plunged
promptly into her affairs to remonstrate,
polemize, and interfere.

None could comprehend her. She stood
alone, but set her mouth doggedly and never
wavered. In her own heart she knew that
Dionysius the weaver stood with her, shoulder to shoulder, and he was a host. Yet a
certain lovely lady of high degree, and most
irreproachably established in life, grown weary
and languid now, and deathly sick at heart,
despite youth, beauty, rank, and wealth,
would, had she but known, have countenanced
Vroni's startling course, — would, had she
but the courage, have done likewise herself.
There was another, also, unchanged in humble fidelity. In our worst and most sorrowful moments we have far-off, unsuspected
friends.

"Art mad, stark mad!" exclaimed Vincenz,
when she announced her purpose.

She shook her head.

"It is impossible!"

"Willst see."

"But it is bad of thee; nay, worse, indecent, to cheat thy children of a father, since I be ready and willing."

She opened her eyes wide with a wonderful silent reply.

"Dost hate me?" he asked in agitation.

"Nay," she answered wearily; "but I should hate thee and myself did I now remain."

"But I love thee, Vroni! I want thee. I'll not have it. I'll prevent it. Art mine by good rights, and I'll keep thee!" he cried in great excitement.

"Dost like me in thy way, I know," she replied with dreary patience; "but 't will pass. Willst get over it, Vincenz, once I be gone."

"I care for none save thee. Every man has his little affairs. But I never loved a woman as I do thee. Art more to me, art different, I swear it!" His voice was warm and strongly agitated.

She moved about, collecting her belongings, and answered nothing.

"'T is thy condition. Willst later come to thy senses;" but her clear and steady gaze disproved his words.

"I'll fetch thy brother," he cried, dismayed. "I'll get the priest to come and reason with thee. I'll get a doctor. 'T is unheard of. The guests bidden, the supper ordered, the marriage hour set, and thou at the last moment meanst not to marry me when I am minded to marry thee and set thee straight and right again. Vroni! Vroni! Canst not see? 'T is mad, 't is craziness!"

The man's face was white and in his voice were deep vibrations which neither she nor he had ever heard.

"Vincenz," she reminded him, "could have slipped away with no word, yet was minded to be honest with thee. Seest I go not in anger. Let us not quarrel. Let me depart in peace. I wish thee well, but, by the living God, I'll never marry thee or house with thee in any wise."

"But why, why?" he cried, trembling and hoarse.

"Have told thee, Vincenz. 'T is the smiling lies. I'll live with them no more, nor suffer my children in their tender years to feed upon such food."

He begged, implored, threatened, flattered, coaxed, reasoned, promised, knelt, and wept. He pleaded well and ill, truth and falsehood.

He fetched others, all who would come, to bombard her: her brother first, and Jakobine, whom this amazing crisis unscrewed from her holy pedestal; the good-hearted landlady who liked the poor young thing and wanted to see her "nicely settled in life, and such a pleasant-spoken, smart young man, to be sure!" Even an old solicitor from a dusty den over the way, to expound law; and, finally, the good priest, whose services were spurned. To their arguments, moral, religious, material, legal, and purely personal, to all their oratory and denunciation, she turned a stony face, and answered seldom a word.

But when Jakobine, voicing the unanimous conviction of the assembly, declared that Vroni, in deliberately refusing the rehabilitating marital establishment, so gallantly proffered by the abandoned bridegroom-elect, and in thus ineradicably confirming her shame, would be guilty of the worst sin of all in her career of open vice, she started up, a flaming spirit in her drawn and pallid face: —

"The sin's not now," she flung back sternly. "The sin was long ago — not now. And, mayhap, Jakobine, mayhap — " long and steadily with those accusing eyes, and with keen intelligence in spite of her wretchedness, she stood scanning her elderly and hostile kinswoman, — "Nay, wouldst never understand. Of what use then to bandy words?" she said quietly, turned away, and dropped into her attitude of passive endurance.

Once again, this time to Melchior, — pathetically pointing out that sooner or later, do what she might, her children would discover her secret, and scorn her, — she retorted, with fiery scorn: —

"Dost think I'll duck and twist and sneak like men? Nay, from my lips and none other shall my children hear the truth, and, if they love me they'll forgive." After a moment, in the pause of consternation that followed her amazing utterance, a poignant tenderness illumined her haggard features, and she added, low and firm: —

"And they will love me!"

What in all this may have stirred the rusty springs of Jakobine's benevolence, compassion, or other occult quality, is indeterminable; but advancing with austere decision from the group, she now proclaimed, and it was much for her: —

"Vroni, willst do the thing thou oughtst,

and marry him forthwith, I'll greet thee
henceforth, and be seen with thee as though
naught unseemly and unsavory e'er had been."

The girl gave her another strange, long
look, and answered slowly: —

"When I do think of thee, I'll try to call
to mind that thou didst speak these words."

Their rhetoric and patience exhausted, in
all sincerity horrified by her utter immorality,
they left her as they found her — inexorable.
Yet one and all hoped and believed with
Vincenz that coming events would break her
obstinacy, and heal her depraved and assuredly
diseased notions.

On the eve of her rejected wedding-day, she
withdrew to an hospital, where, in her careless days, she had once seen women walking
and sewing in a large garden. She had still
some time to wait, but was much broken in
strength, and sadly in need of care and refuge.
So she, too, walked and sat in the pleasant
garden, and fashioned the weaver's fine linen
into tiny garments, and suffered various acute
miseries of soul and body attendant upon the
birth of her boy, Dion.

Turning again yearningly toward ancient
landmarks, desiring, too, in case of her death,

to recommend to mercy her poor little Nita, she wrote from the hospital to her brother Sebastian and to Sister Corona some rather sturdy little letters, for even now she was not good at whimpering. She took her pen in hand to pen them the usual amenities: she stated that, *Gottlob*, she was very well, and hoped they were the same and also enjoying very good health. After which, she penned them the naked truth. In few words she stated her case, — her past, her present, her contemplated future; and she humbly entreated their pardon.

Sebastian responded with fulminations, and exhorted — nay, commanded — her to marry Vincenz Berg. The shadowy nun, no less, from faultless but loveless heights, adjured her erring sister to take the one step of reparation. Melchior journeyed to the convent, and the three in council indited more letters, in which the worthy Sebastian disposed somewhat freely of the wrath of God, and flung into his utterances an ex-cathedra *pectus*.

Vroni grew whiter as she read. It was all quite true. She was a sinner, an outcast, a disgrace to them, and the name was honest save for her. She was bad, and they were

good.   Yet she knew no shadow of swerving.
She wrote no more.

Melchior appeared once, as accredited envoy
of the outraged family, a dreary ambassador,
visibly shrivelled as to affection, a mere tottering hanger-on and slave of conventionality.
Hearing her curt last word, he groaned and
went out.   In due time, with what in fact
might almost be termed mundane promptness,
Sister Corona and Sebastian wrote they would
pray for Vroni's soul, but never see her in the
flesh again — except as the wife of Vincenz
Berg — which was practically an eternal farewell, their ultimate destination beyond the
tomb being so remote from hers.   In conclu-
sion, Sebastian, for a man engaged chiefly in
agricultural pursuits, executed a very fair
species of Bull of Excommunication, — none,
save a certain great tragedian, ever better
launched the curse of Rome.

Vincenz prowled anxiously around the hospital, where he was denied admittance.   In-
furiated by her course, infatuated with her
still, more keenly alive to her worth now
that he had lost her, wounded too, for the
first time in his vanity of conquering hero he
vowed he would marry her yet.   It was but a

freak of illness, he jauntily assured Melchior,
and even boasted with vague suggestiveness
of tidings from the hospital, messages of contrition and renewed constancy. Melchior
feebly responded they would hope for the
best. His sympathies, everybody's sympathies, were with Berg, who obviously was the
injured party. He had erred. Well, young
men would be young men. But he was handsomely and generously eager to make amends.
He was behaving well, and he stood for law,
order, good citizenship, morality, and religion.
Wretched girls all over the world were left
in the lurch. One was used to the trite spec-
tacle, and they had but themselves to thank
for their misery. But this novel turning of
the tables upon the man, the unique, unconscious irony of Vroni's attitude, naturally
roused a startled indignation.

Praying she might never look upon his face
again, Vroni, still pale and weak, her baby in
her arms, stole away by night to Hexenfels.
What it cost her, thus to confront her village,
would have nerved an army. But the village
folk, passive and shy toward the changed and
citified girl, molested her not at all. Whatever were her sister Marie's thoughts, she was

a gentle creature, and uttered no reproach. Old Tante Ursula was less reticent. Yet even she, after days of aggrieved and Christian denunciation, gradually got an inkling of the amazing truth that this sombre, resolute girl-woman of twenty, mute under attack, unmoved by argument as the great crag by butterflies, making with stern dignity and much foresight the most minute arrangements for the well-being of her two unsanctioned babies, could be, in spite of facts and the explicit assertions of her wrathful brothers, no light o' love.

"'T is ever the same little Vroni," mused the old woman, in secret, "the naughtiest but the dearest of them all."

Although never by word or look condoning the girl's reprehensible and lawless course in refusing to wipe the foul stain from the family honor and her poor helpless children, Tante Ursula, rigidly devout yet mellowed by great age, finally abandoned scathing oratory, was good to Vroni during her brief stay, and in her absence spoke many an indulgent word for her, while those two little waifs became the old woman's all-absorbing care, her consolation, and her joy.

The girl-mother, in manner matter-of-fact and unemotional, ironclad in stubborn peasant pride, gave never a sign of the storms and agonies within. But the Witch-Tooth, the pile of fagots, the crooked plum-trees, the forest, the corn-fields, and the great night-winds could have told another story. Yet she gained strength wandering among the old haunts, and from her mountain fastnesses took with keen eyes, sound judgment and indomitable tenacity, her new life-bearings.

The babies were best off here; therefore, for the present, here should they stay. Hungering for them afar off would be a part of her punishment. Here they would have pure air and sure kindness, be screened from unfriendly notice, — indeed, amid Marie's brood, quite inconspicuous. Every Easter she would come to them, oftener if possible, but that was scarcely probable; for all her earnings were spent, she must stay at her post and work hard. The regular monthly payment would be cheering to Marie, who saw coin rarely, tailoring not being a lucrative business in Hexenfels. Vroni reckoned what she must earn annually, what use for her own bare needs, what for their comfort and growing

necessities, — more and more each year, — and
what she ought to set aside in the savings
bank against the time they would need it
when learning their trades, or against an evil
day.

From marriage she had excluded herself
forever, had broken with tradition and training, and wrenched herself loose from the close-
clinging notions and prejudices dear to her
class.   The entire significance of this painful
process was even now unrevealed to her; but
each day threw fresh light upon the long,
hard, lonely, endless road stretching on before
her.   But whether delusion or revelation she
believed that she was walking it with the
direct blessing and sympathy of Dionysius
the weaver, and to him, grievously far away
yet nearer than the uncomprehending visible
world, she confided her most trivial plans.

The great winds of the home country not
only blew new life and strength into her, but
seemed to cleanse her inner being, and inter-
pose their purifying breath between her soul
and that evil time in ever-receding distance.
Yet when she clasped both children in her
arms, Anita winsome, sunny, a palpable delight, while Dion lay a dark, soft mystery

upon her breast, she was conscious of bliss transcending bitterness; and not to elude remorse and shame or torture a thousand-fold more cruel than that she had endured, would she annul the two fateful years that had borne these precious fruits. From them, her reproach among men, proceeded a sacred joy and a lofty purpose, and with a deep and hitherto unknown awe she marvelled at the subtle shaping hand of destiny.

"God willing, I will keep them straight, father. They shall be wholesome-minded like to thee. Nita shall not be left alone, a young thing, wild and ignorant of life. For her protection there is that which she shall hear, — nay, I will not shrink. And Dion shall speak the truth. I undertake it, father. Thank God, they have thy eyes, not his. Thank thee, my mother, and my master, I know my work and can support them."

Thus the great saints of her private calendar came, belated, to their dues, and she blessed them daily for their good works, as she, mournful yet resolute, left her beloved mountains — thrice dear, now that they guarded her treasures — and entered upon the grave and weary years of her atonement.

Meanwhile, a lovely lady of high degree, upon whom the winds of heaven were not suffered to blow roughly, whose marriage was immaculate before Church and State, moaned in her heart, unceasingly : —

"I cannot dig, to beg I am ashamed. I have not learned to work. I could not teach the youngest child. I know not whither to go. I am too cowardly to die. Yet there is nothing I would fear to do, or suffer, or attempt, with Eck. But he is silent, and Africa is far. My life is hideous. It is a monstrous thing that girls are left so blind. Had I but known!"

And none at Court wore toilettes such as hers, and her three brothers kept racers.

XV

PROMINENT among Vroni's unforeseen trials was the extreme persistence of Vincenz Berg's pursuit. On his account she left comfortable situations and pleasant towns. He traced her course, followed her from house to house, from city to city, compromised her among strangers, and agitated her with odious scenes. He went down on his knees and implored her to marry him, whined, wailed, shouted, swore, and promised amendment beyond her loftiest ideals. Doubtless for the most part he was in his way sincere, although he usually appeared in somewhat alcoholic temper.

He had lost his excellent position and was evidently drinking habitually. For both of these misfortunes he reproached her; she was, he said, destroying him. Materially changed he was, unquestionably; one had not imagined a weak man, thwarted, could react with such force. Sometimes he threatened to blow his brains out and hers and the babies'. She could not see him thus demoralized without a haunting sense of guilty responsibility, as an unwilling accomplice in his ruin. Altogether he succeeded often enough in making of her a miserable, sickened woman, and spiritless until she spurred herself on with the thought of the sanctity of the cause for which she was fighting.

A frightened woman she became,—even she, — dreading a bright market on a sunny morning, glancing furtively about as she crossed herself and knelt upon entering her church. Formerly, with the frolic expectancy of Hide and Seek, or Catch, she had been alert for the whimsical suddenness of that jaunty apparition. Her pantomime of quick, exhaustive scrutiny of portal, passage, and arcade was still the same, but, ah! the terrible irony of the essential change in her informing spirit.

After a couple of years, however, this terror persecuted her no longer. Months passed in which she neither saw nor heard him. Later, vague rumors of him reached her. He had married a Protestant—was rich—was divorced—had gone to America. Then at last she breathed freely once more and found her full strength.

In a monetary sense, she prospered beyond her hopes. Her deposits in the savings bank were encouraging, her payments to Marie regular and liberal, the children well-fed and well-clothed. When, every Easter, Vroni appeared in Hexenfels, plainly clad, grave, and self-possessed, the repose and determination upon her handsome face, together with the impressiveness of her severe little matronly bonnet, were gradually and subtly tending toward reinstating her in public esteem, — giving her, as it were, a not ignoble place apart, and almost the vicarious dignity, say, of a widow.

"'T is the money," thought Vroni, shrewdly and without bitterness, for she was beginning to observe manifold phases of life. Yet it could but soothe her cruelly wounded pride to be treated with growing respect by her home people.

Each spring Anita ran to her with open arms, was glad, pretty, winning, and proud to have a mother. The child was docile, blithe, and full of prattle, sat over-young but with decorum upon Father Aloysius's knee, and never endangered the family spoon. But Dion, scowling and shy, would watch Vroni long with beautiful gloomy eyes in which her

poor heart read reproach, repulsed her, would
not call her mother, would yield, she found,
to no caress or entreaty; but, left to his own
instincts, after two or three days of her
martyrdom, would seize her on a sudden and
cling with speechless and passionate intensity.

" 'T is well I cannot see them twice a year.
The parting is too cruel, and saps the strength
that I do greatly need for them," she would
say grimly to herself, gird up her loins, and
stride forth upon her battlefield.

Of men she voluntarily saw as little as
possible. But although she shunned merrymakings and all places that could steal a
penny from the inheritance of her children,
she was too handsome and too unique to escape man's notice, at times his intrusiveness.
She knew fatally well what in her case even
the best of it was worth, for this was one of
the special phases of human nature her lot
had forced her to investigate. Some men
wanted merely to amuse themselves. Others
were honestly attracted and meant marriage,
until by chance a flying hint of her misfortunes reached them, when they forthwith felt
justified in approaching her with lax language
and revolting designs, — such as she being

obviously fair game. She made short work of them. The flash of her eye and her grim contempt struck like blows.

But once she almost liked a man. He was a friendly, manly, intelligent fellow with a record for bravery. She saw him growing fond of her and eager to declare himself; so she nerved herself to intercept him with her tale, that is, with its resultant facts, and saw him blanch and slink away. For though brave enough before guns, he, too, dared not face the world.

She had indeed abjured marriage, but not of her own freewill all kindly human intercourse, and had been glad of his companionship and good sense. For with her brutal disillusions and her steadily ripening mind she had become mortally weary of her women associates' incessant chatter of sweethearts, and breathless estimate of the chances of securing this or that man as life's ultimate aim and triumph. So this defection gave her a brief pang, left her wiser, and it may be a trifle harder.

Neither he nor her sorrier suitors had the brain to perceive that for the long, uphill pull of matrimony, the unblemished lamb with a large dowry whom they all were seeking to better their fortunes was not, even from the worldly and practical point of view, where they based all calculations, comparable to this able and intelligent creature, tried in the fires of adversity, finely tempered for any conflict, and possessed of heart qualities of surpassing richness and purity.

Fools that they were, they beheld only her pretty oval face, her brown and ruddy skin, her young smile, for that she kept, — a smile is a thing that dies hard; her eyes, her form, her step, her charm, and over all, the ugly stain upon her reputation which, according to their low and cruel creed, made her fair prey for the meanest of their noble fellowship.

Open-eyed, viewing much, one fated to be confronted ever by distinct and manifold experiences, she would cry at moments in withering scorn: —

"Truly, men folk, high and low, have much to learn of sense and decency," then meekly, — "and women, too, alas! Yet cowards are the men, despite their swagger. 'T is well we four crave naught of them."

Isolating herself habitually, and for entertainment thrown wholly upon her own resources, she now began to read, at first with exceeding effort, an evening paper. It filled her with impatience to sit still at it, and the novel mental exertion induced the phenomenon of curiously cramped and restless legs. Frequently she laid it aside, only to take it up again and regard it with frowning speculation.

"Ha! 'T were a blame on me could I strain naught of its sense into my brain-pan, when the fat Vallade butler did draw the whole strength out of the print and never blink."

It was arduous digging, but she persevered. 'T was at least, she reflected, no harm and might sometime be a bit useful to the children. Every night she had perhaps an hour free before bedtime, sometimes more. Slowly and painfully she established the habit of consecutive reading,—a very different thing from being able and not unwilling to read whatever sporadic bit was strictly necessary in the line of one's cooking. The love for this employment was naturally of still slower growth, but also evolved in time. Her evening paper, at first so impenetrable, became familiar and easy reading of which she finally made her choice with almost the aplomb of the butler.

She took the leaders with tremendous seri-

ousness and seized the heart of them — when
they possessed one. At length she turned to
books, choosing by chance a volume of essays
noticed in her paper. The style was clear;
the themes, relating to human intercourse,
within her mental grasp. Words strange to
her she looked up in her dictionary. She
found a " lot of *Kauderwelsch*, but the talk was
brave sense." She continued to read thoughtful books. She had considerably more than
three hundred and sixty-five hours in a year
for her modest researches in literature, since
on every other Sunday she could command
nearly half a day. In three hundred and sixty-
five hours is time enough, however, for various things.

One autumn morning, nearly five years after
Melchior had rushed groaning from the hospital,
he was drearily airing his royal equine charges,
when he met a young woman with a white cap,
a long white apron, a big brown basket, a
swift step, and a vivid face not easy to forget.

Instinctively he drew up his horses, and she
stopped short.

" Vroni ! " he cried, glancing quickly around
to see if they were observed, but it was a
rather lonely street.

"*Grüss Gott*, Melchior," she returned coolly.

"*Na* — Vroni!"

"'T is my name."

"Whence comst thou?" he stammered.

"From market, as thou seest."

"Knowst that be not my meaning. Where hast thou whiled this long, long time?"

"In all four winds' quarters," she answered nonchalantly.

"What doing?"

"Earning my bread. Hadst been minded to know aught of me, couldst have knocked at our good Marie's door, eh?"

"Hast really come back, Vroni?"

"Ha, what thinkst? Mayhap I be a ghost."

"Art not wedded?" he asked timidly,

"Nay — thanks and praise ten thousandfold to God."

"And art in a respectable house?"

"As to that I know not, meanings being many a time contrariwise 'twixt me and thee. 'T is a house with a brave appetite. For that I cook. 'T is a house with gold in its strong box. Of that I have my dues. More I ask not."

He gazed at her in wonder, curiosity, and

no little excitement, strangely glad in spite of himself. His life was dull and disappointing, and Jakobine palled. There stood his reprobate sister, pretty as a picture and quite at her ease.

"'Tis most amazing — and I'll not deny it pleaseth me not ill to greet thee," he admitted, vaguely apologetic.

"Fine thanks," she dryly returned. "Art little changed, I mark, without or within."

"Thou, Vroni, how didst chance then to return?"

"Oh, the family where I cook did of late move hither. I was not loath. The town did ever suit me fairly well."

She greatly puzzled him with the cool negligence of her manner. It seemed to him he was called upon to remonstrate, but a gleam that daunted him was lurking in her eye.

"What family might it be?" he demanded with anxiety.

Serious and deliberate, she replied: —

"'Tis a family that makes bold to call itself by name Prince Uhl-Rheda."

"O Lord!" exclaimed Melchior, and for the first time in his official career was guilty of the enormity of dropping his whip.

She gravely picked it up and handed it to him.

"Uhl-Rheda!" he gasped.

"'T is the name that I did speak."

"Art there since when?"

"Nigh on two years, — after much wandering and vexing change less to my mind. Always before they 'd had a *chef*. But I," she quoted calmly, "am quite as good a cook and less extravagant and variable. 'T is the message that did come down to me from the gracious *Herrschaft*."

"Vroni, do they suspect thy — history?"

Her eyes clouded ominously, but she still curbed her tongue.

"Did inquire naught concerning their past doings nor they of mine. 'T were scarce princely to pry into such humble matters. I cook to suit their palates, have a head for reckoning, and cheat them not. With that they are content, and rightly so. I pray thee, be thou likewise."

In her restraint was a warning a wise man might have heeded.

"Seemst to sit rarely firm in thy saddle," he murmured.

"'T is as thou sayst, Melchior."

" 'T is all most strange. Hast heard aught from Sebastian? Hath he forgiven thee?"

She waited some moments, her nostrils dilating, her breathing short and quick, her gaze averted, before saying low and strenuously: —

"*I have forgiven him.*"

At this, what Melchior called his principles began to bubble: —

"Nay, Vroni, so mayst a maid like thee not speak of one who is the head of all of us, and of truly holy life. 'T is grievous, on my soul, to find thee bold when modesty and lamentation would better suit thy case. When I do mark thy carelessness, and mind me of those two unhappy children, thy shame and my own —"

Strong, resolute, and fiery, her spirit leaped in her face. She put the basket on the pavement, took a step forward, and with an imperious gesture stopped him: —

"Thou, Melchior, I'll have a straight word with thee, here and now. I pray thee, hearken. Of thy sermons I am minded to hear naught. Art thou disposed to give me of thy converse, thou shalt henceforth speak naught to me thou mightst not in thy civil manners to a stranger. Art set neither by God Almighty nor by His

Majesty the King to tutor me, and how it doth look inside me is truly mine own care, and thine in no wise. Mark that, I pray thee.

"I grant I did ye all great wrong; but in return what did ye, my two brothers, but leave me to die like a dog by the roadside or fall to a worse fate, were I so inclined? Therefore I'll brook no word from thee, for 't is not in my nature. Let each square his sins with his own conscience and cry quits with the other. I ask naught of thee. I need thee not. Hast heard?

"I mind me, thou didst even now let fall some words unseemly to mine ears, — 't is of them we now do speak. I pray thee, favor me with thy attention. Seest, Melchior, I am the mother of two beautiful children, and I have money in the bank for them, and I can cook to-day in the palace of thy royal master, the King, if so I do desire. My way I've made alone. 'T was not a way of daisies. 'T was hard toil, hard thought, hard fighting, and much else bitter hard of which I speak not. Do thou not mind that; 't is my matter. But that which I do pray thee to heed well, — 't is this my present speech.

"Sebastian, as doth freely please him, will

gather artichokes and pray his angry prayers.
'T is naught to me. 'T is air. Thou, Melchior,
mayst look English at me from thy box. It
doth move me not at all. Can myself look
English, or worse still, so that be needed. Have
got beyond thee, Melchior, in that I fear naught.
'T is standing alone has done it, — against the
world and for my Nita and my Dion.

"And once for all I say to thee I shame
me not for them — no more. For all wrong-
doing in the past, God is my judge. But for
my children I now know no shame; nor mayst
thou dare again to speak that word and their
names in one breath. Hast heard, Melchior.

"Am proud of them. Will not permit one
syllable, one look, one thought flung at them,
as if they had no place or right upon this
earth. Ha! 't is pity, truly, thou canst not
take 'the beauties' in thine arms and see
them, sweet and shy-like, spy at thee yet with
the father's own deep eyes. They 'd freshen
thee, my poor old Melchior, thou who didst ever
in thy secret heart long for a little child to
father and to love.

"Yet seest, ere that thou touchest them,
thou needst must honor every hair of their
dear heads, — and me, because I 'm their

mother. Shouldst ever crave to see me, Melchior, *on these terms*, shallst find me. I bear no grudge; can welcome thee to-morrow, and greet even thy Jakobine in friendly wise. But if our hands do ever meet, we 'll stand on this ground that I now do say to thee, and on no other. Otherwise — English! Have spoken. Thou hast heard. Wish thee good-day."

Taking up her basket, she turned her back upon the petrified King's coachman and marched off briskly.

XVI

ALONE, as was her habit, grave, self-contained, Vroni went to Vespers in the church where Vincenz used to kneel, too close, beside her and look askance at her in prayer-time; where at the portals he had waited with his half-smiling stare, and from whence he followed to intrude his sleek selfishness into the cool sanctuary of her childlike thought: in that church where too she had sought and found more than earthly help in the hour of her agony, and made her peace with Dionysius the weaver, who she was convinced had never left her since.

In sharp self-scrutiny and self-abasement, she re-lived every epoch of that fateful time; for if she confronted the world valiantly, before the tribunal of her own soul she extenuated nothing, and was retentive of every pang she had suffered and of every hateful scene in which she had figured during the period of her gay shamelessness.

It was unsafe to forget, she meditated, upon her knees; not always to dwell upon it, for that weakened her elasticity, yet never to let one line of it grow faint. For in her, somewhere, buried deep and out of sight, was a wild strain yet. She felt it leap when there was music on a sudden, and sometimes, God forgive her, when men's eyes looked kind on her, and men's eyes, beholding her, were but too apt to look too kind. It was then as though her heart were a strange, strong, free thing, — glad, dare-devil, and gypsyish, — caring for naught on earth save its own whim. And if this sleeping wildness should wake again and rise up and seize her, what would become of her Nita and her Dion? So she still shunned music, mirth, and men, although the steadily increasing sum in the savings bank would have justified a little relaxation. It was in truth an ascetic life she was leading, but she called it by no high name.

Humbly thankful for what she had overcome, for what she had gained of strength, she left the church, and in the early autumn dusk ascended the winding path of the little park, stopped at sorrowful stations in her reminiscence, and prayed her prayers and loved her children.

"For some cause I do fear naught for my
Nita-le, maid though she be; yet many a time
I'm grieving, knowing not what's in my
Dion's being, or whence his mood apart.
The Marie says ofttimes he's rarely far off
in himself and like no child.   Pray God
there be not in his blood too much of *him*.
Truly Melchior leans not in likeness toward
the father; nor doth Marie nor Sebastian; nor
I myself, save in the outward features, though
't was the father's meaning — loving me and
knowing not what should arrive of ill — that
he did ever fairly spy himself in me.   'T is
odd one can count surer on a dumb beast's
heritage than on a human child's.   My Dion
doth torment me.   So there be in him of
Vincenz's strain, I pray it be but moderate
large, and like to Vincenz only when he was
a little curly headed child, — so much, no
more.   Yet many a time with aching heart
I tremble for my little lad — for my Dion
was the sin."

At her next dusky station she stood some
time.   She was resolved to live no longer
banished from the children; and, Vincenz
gone, she had no fear.   Their sweet baby-
hood she had for their gain foregone and

mourned unceasingly though showing outwardly a savage fortitude. But the time was
come for her to have them near. She felt
they now imperatively needed her. In the
spring Dion, after finally deigning to emerge
from his stony reserve, to recognize and asso-
ciate with her familiarly, had said solemnly:

" Dost while long in the *Unterland*."

She endeavored to explain, in terms suited
to his baby-comprehension, the causes of the
infrequency of her visits.

Sombre and unconvinced, his great eyes re-
buked her: —

" Whilst long," he persisted, frowning.

She must have them; yet how, where, under
what conditions she was wholly unable even
to conjecture. So profoundly lost in thought
was she that she perceived but by degrees the
voices, words, at last the paramount meaning
of a man and woman who had approached and
were speaking low and rapidly behind a clump
of trees — the woman hardly above her sighing breath.

" Ha, 't is the park-business, and another
fool like me."

The man's voice urged and pleaded — low,
warm, most strenuous.

"'T is pity. There's awful foolishtry in God's brave world. Would I could stop her! Would I could hold one single poor maid back from the blind rush I myself did make. But, alas, I cannot! 'T is to men maids hearken ever. She's minded to run off with him. 'T is plain. A lady — awfully fond but breaking quite in twain for trouble, love, and fear. Poor thing! Hear her sob. Do I mistake not, — he has a fairly honest voice, even to mine own cold ears that be not over favorable to such as he. Where, long since, did I hear that voice?"

Listening more intently, she caught a few clear words from the woman.

Swift steps startled the lovers; from the gloom a form emerged, dropped at the lady's feet and clasped her knees.

"Nay, Comtesse Nelka, nay!"

Eck Flemming seized the intruder's shoulder.

"Don't speak roughly to her. It is only Vroni."

"Do not be afraid," poor Nelka, trembling from head to foot, said sweetly; "you know I always liked you, Vroni, and I've wondered what had become of you in this long time." She put her head protectingly on Vroni's head.

" Get up, Vroni, you have nothing to fear where
I am."

" 'Tis for the gracious comtesse only and
alone that I do fear me. I overheard. Comtesse, 'tis sheer impossible. Oh, go away, Herr
Eck, go far from her!" Vroni cried fiercely.

" Vroni, my good girl, let go the comtesse;
come to your senses; get up on your feet and
leave us. Our affairs do not concern you.
You forget yourself strangely."

Again he sought to separate her from Nelka.

But Vroni, kneeling still, one arm thrown
round the comtesse, half turned to face him,
and with ungovernable feeling exclaimed:

" Me, most of all do they concern: and 'tis
just because I remember of myself that I do
speak. And I will speak, and you shall listen,
Herr Eck Flemming."

He made an impatient movement and ex-
clamation.

" Come, Nelka, let us go on," he said.

" Nay, for I 'll follow," retorted Vroni, low
and vehement, rising quickly. " You cannot
shake me off. I 'll stop at naught. I will
alarm them all, so there be need. Will go myself to Count Vallade and the countess. Will
telegraph to the Counts Benno, Knod, and

Waldemar. I 'll not tell Baron Frege, for he shall never know."

"Vroni! Vroni!" moaned Nelka, aghast.

The girl turned, and, in her old impulsive ardent way, kissed the comtesse's hands.

"She 's crazy," muttered Flemming.

"'T is not the first time I 'm so called, yet ever, to my comfort, when I be most sound of sense. Herr Eck, I pray your pardon if I be sharp and rude. I am not minded to do such harsh things as I spake. I but said, mark you, if there be need."

"I do not doubt your intentions are excellent," he replied, with authoritative kindness; "but there is nothing whatever you can say which we wish to hear. I must insist upon your going at once. You must see yourself it is an unheard of piece of presumption, meddlesome, in short, to the last degree, and I 'll ask you to have the kindness to go off."

"Herr Eck," she said quite gently, "that I am a servant and you a learned young gentleman is mayhap what is in your mind. But for that I care not. It is air. 'T is to your heart I have a word to say."

"Speak, Vroni," said the lady, "I wish it. We both will listen."

" Herr Eck, I pray you to look back and to remember. Were, if I err not, a little orphan-boy, son of Count Vallade's oldest friend; friends as lads, youths, and men, were they. Not all great men at Court are faithful. But the count took you into his home, sent you to the best schools, gladdened your holidays, let you miss naught, was proud of your brave talent. You were like one of his own sons, save hardier in body, stronger at book-learn-ing, and honester of heart, — leastwise, 't was so believed. 'T is many a year of goodness you have to thank him for, and he is a gray-haired man and sorely careworn, and the one joy that gladdens him, 't is the gracious Comtesse Nelka. Speak I true words, Herr Eck? "

The man was silent. He forgot whose was this strange and penetrating voice in the dark.

" And the young counts? *Na*, I know, but 't is chiefly the empty-headed way they 're bred. Fond of you are they every one. I once did overhear Count Waldemar say Herr Eck was his ' blood-brother,' the one man that he did really care for. They were your good comrades years and years. They shared half

and half with you when you had naught save
for the Vallades. Truly they be fast and
senseless-selfish; they do live the life and go
the pace, and howe'er else they may name
their pretty doings; and whatsoever bad, mad
freak is on the wind, they grasp it with both
hands; and with women sheer cruel, as most
doth please you men, Herr Eck Flemming;
but if there be one thing on earth these three
gay brothers believe in and hold high, it is
the gracious Comtesse Nelka. Is it true, Herr
Eck?"

"It is true, Vroni," he muttered hoarsely.

"Herr Eck, she is an angel. Leave her
one. She's miserable; but she'll know worse
misery if she does this thing. 'T is your
meaning to gladden and to care for her most
softly; but you have but one little span of life,
and what if you should die? What then?
How would she live, she and her children?
For though you think not of it, and she, poor
gracious lady, less, 't is fitting I at least do
now remind you, there be always children
following such steps, — which is a thing of
great import, not likely to be put aside. In
all things there is a giving and a taking. 'T is
surely fair to reckon both; and in your mind,

which doth possess so much of learning, to weigh well if you do give enough to cover all that which you do take from her."

It was impossible longer to spurn this un-bidden counsellor whose soft and solemn voice so fast, so eager yet controlled, now in the sturdy phrase of the Rough Alp, now with a book-word but recently made her own, con-tinued its appeal, and hardly stopped except when some passer-by briefly approached too near, or when, for but an instant, she seemed to seek her argument.

Leaning against a tree, Flemming stood silent and heard the woman pleading in the darkness as if she were his conscience incar-nate, so often had he himself dwelt weightily upon every point which she accentuated; yet he flung his arm round Nelka and held her close as if against the world. She, sobbing no more, quite motionless, her cheek upon his breast, listened and wished that she were dead.

"See, Herr Eck, it is not possible the thing you want — not for you two. She cannot bear rough things. She never learned to work. Hardship would kill her. But truly 't is not these that be the worst to bear. Do you sup-

pose the gracious Comtesse Nelka is one that
could know a moment's peace did her father
follow her, waking and sleeping, with stern
eyes turned from her? And your own dead
father who, dying, left you to his friend?
And the Countess Vallade?"

Flemming gave a violent start, but Nelka
laid her hand across his lips.

"Ah, yes, Herr Eck, I know. Ofttimes we
serving-folk, without much striving, do spy
more out mayhap than the *Herrschaft* fancies.
'T is not fitting to bespeak it narrowly, but
of some matters I did chance to hear a hint,
and truly 't was most grievous. Knew I then
what now I know, 't is I myself would have
oped my mouth wide, fearing naught. But
five years gone, much did entangle me, nor
did my *Herrschaft's* manners seem by good
rights my concern. Truly a wrong was done
you, and a greater wrong my Comtesse Nelka
— for all your lives. Yet how about the
years, Herr Eck, when she did never wrong
you, when she did love you and was good to
you, and never let you, at least, feel her great
pride? Ah, Herr Eck, it is not wise to dwell
upon our wrongs alone. 'T is I may say it,
being prone to it myself."

"Oh, gracious Comtesse Nelka," and now was Vroni little less than wonderful in her protecting tenderness through which throbbed her own stern sorrow, "it greatly hurts and stings, when the world jeers one, and folk worse than one was ever at one's worst do have a sort of right to tread one underfoot and call foul names. And it doth hurt like knives when one's own do turn from one, and brothers curse, — for there be they who truly curse in prayer. 'T is years until one, plodding slow, teeth set, doth learn to bear it, and make as though one careth not, — but one careth, and will ever care, till one's death day.

"Even they that be rough and tough and used to toil, and stout to fight their way and let naught show upon the countenance, die many deaths of grief, of loneliness, of hopelessness, of misery and shame. And, my gracious comtesse, my pretty, pretty Comtesse Nelka, with her soft white ways, and her gentle heart — *ach Gott, ach Gott!*"

"You see, dear Eck," murmured Nelka, piteously, "it is as I told you. I have not strength to go. I have not strength to remain. I am worthless."

Flemming held her in his close grasp, yet spoke no word of comfort. A hot conflict was raging in his soul.

"Strength to remain has my gracious Comtesse Nelka! Strength not to stab her father's heart, and not to wound all these people, that, whatever they do lack, — truly, 't is much, — love her the best they know. Herr Eck speaks not, but, in his great wisdom and his learning and his pity, are his thoughts good again.

"See. 'T is that you two, just you two, may not murder the peace of mind of them that have been good to you; and bad again, 't is true, but good was most and longest. Then there are others. I pray your pardon that I do speak of these when your hearts so do swell and burst with your own griefs. Yet I do make so bold, being moved strongly in my thought, to say there be on all sides little fools of working girls, of the sort I myself used to be, five or six years agone; mayhap not evil-hearted, but empty in the head — lacking instruction — and chiefly wanting they know not what, reaching out after a little joy.

"A thousand such may go astray and the

world is none the wiser. But, Comtesse Nelka!
If she did sacrifice all else and go away with
you, Herr Eck, she with her great name and
everything that others lack and crave, — beauty
and money, and a rich, soft life, — then all the
little working girls would say: 'See! She
had everything this world can give, yet did
but that she liked. Then why not we?'
So she'd push scores of them down — down
so far that few would ever crawl up again;
and no wonder, for God knows the crawling
up is bitter hard, and the hands that fain
would thrust one down again, and deeper
down, — they do fail never more.

"And who will remember the comtesse is
innocent and good? And who will say you
were like brother and sister all your lives, and
grievously mishandled, in that 'twas no fair
play that did rend you in twain? Who will
believe, Herr Eck, that you be honest; that
you would die a thousand deaths rather than
hurt her; that you do stand there now this
instant, in silence, with your heart like to a
live coal in your breast, and mad with grief,
not for yourself alone, though you do love
her with your strong man's love, but likewise because you do behold her in misery

and grievousness of life and fain would save and comfort her?

"But none will care for that. She will be lumped with the bad and lost and shameless ones. 'T is monstrous. 'T is not sense. But true it is. As if she ever could be aught but clean and white! But the world stops not to draw lines, be there a body to hoot and stone. Truly, 't is a rare fool-world for women folk, and that's the kernel of my thought.

"Nor do I now speak of the right and wrong of things. Ha! Were there but you twain, and he who evilly did buy her! My meanings as to what sin be and be not are my own, and none such as noisy tongues do bray in herds. Mayhap, I could say more, not illy founded in my reason, and in God's sight truth, though ten thousand worlds do blunder ere their wisdom teeth be grown; mayhap, indeed, one day, to my gracious Comtesse Nelka only, — nay, 't is enough! It may not be.

"Herr Eck, I do declare it be not possible, *not possible*, that you, having a great heart and wisdom beyond common folk, do hurt beyond repair so many men and women, and most our gracious and beloved Comtesse Nelka. 'T is why, in your greatheartedness, you now most stoutly do propose to save her, — you that be her other brother, her truest brother of them all."

Speechless and close the two stood, and in the stillness of the night, over their wrath, their sorrow, their love, despair, and passion; over their poignant yearning for happiness, hovered the mighty angel of renunciation, his broad wings drawing ever nearer, his message imminent.

Slowly, with lingering movement, Nelka lifted her sad head; softly she withdrew from Flemming's sheltering arm; reluctantly she unclasped her clinging hands and stood apart. He suffered it.

The church clock struck the half hour.

Nelka, dazed and chilly of soul, murmured brokenly: —

" They will be wondering — expecting me. The carriage was to meet me at my father's."

" I will take the gracious comtesse to her father's."

As if waking from a dream to hideous reality, and unable to bear the burden of her days, Nelka, with a little shuddering cry, sprang to refuge, and he gathered her in his arms and murmured, desperately, in a sudden relapse of resolution: —

" It is reason, what she says, not love.   It is truth; there are other truths, strong and masterful.   Speak the word, Nelka.   My life is yours, yours the decision.   Command.   I obey. God knows I would not hurt you, dear, yet only come with me and we will — "

" To-morrow," broke in the lady, faintly, " we will say the rest."

" To-morrow," he rejoined in profound agitation, " is my last day.   Speak now, for God's sake, Nelka, — and come, ah, come ! "

Vroni sank back, and grasped a railing for support.   In her suspense it seemed that all was lost.   The tide had turned, her strength was spent.

" To-morrow," trembled slowly from Nelka's lips, " you and I, my dearest, will say good-bye."

In the hush that followed, sounded a fine bugle-note calling a brave man to the last charge in a lost but holy cause.

" Nay, Herr Eck, speak now the farewell word, and leave to-night — having a great heart."

Withdrawing a few steps, Vroni turned away and waited.

XVII

BEER foamed in great tankards, the roast goose was succulent and brown. At every table in the large well-lighted room were men and women in gala mood, and Vroni sat, at last, between Melchior and Jakobine, flanked by a group of pre-eminently respectable old servants of the palace, all smoking strenuously.

Vroni retreating, Melchior and Jakobine had pursued. She not heeding them, they had shown themselves disposed to serve her. Her bold declaration of independence, together with her appreciated position in the household of a prince, had won them. She had anticipated this result from the day she valiantly belabored her brother and went home to weep for homesickness. When after some weeks of deliberation Melchior came with Jakobine's invitation for this special evening, Vroni accepted with the quiet air of one inured to family amenities. Afterwards she frowned, smiled, and sighed:

"The worth of it know I full well. Never

mind. 'T is mayhap better so, better some
day for Nita and my Dion. Then 't is my
brother after all be said, and when I do
gaze upon his sad sheep face, my heart
doth mildly speak for him."

So she sat clear-eyed, serene, among the
royal liveries, at the most distinguished table,
where sententious politics rolled forth in the
most truly monarchical spirit, and the shining
personages over-conscious of their dignity
were less merry than their simpler brethren.

Vroni spoke little, was quiet, content, withdrawn into herself. It was the first time in
years she had participated in so much dis-
sipation. She heard the heavy wisdom of
the men; and had she desired could have re-
futed it, for her dogged reading and uncowed
thought had led her far beyond their plati-
tudes. Melchior was at heart well pleased,
and Jakobine grumbled less than her wont,
for Vroni was sedate and still, stared neither
right nor left, and wore a bonnet like a lady's,
with not a feather or a flower on it. Her
dress too was severely plain. So was the
Queen's that morning when Melchior drove
her out. His affection, long smothered and
deadened, was reviving, and he was pleasure-

ably conscious of magnanimity. It occurred to him it would do no harm to mention to Sebastian that Vroni gave full satisfaction at Prince Uhl-Rheda's, and that she made a distinctly favorable impression upon his own esteemed colleagues and associates. There could be no doubt Vroni was swimming along in the full stream of social recognition.

The room became more crowded, the tobacco fumes denser, beer flowed continually, animation increased.

"'T is wondrous strange," mused Vroni, "that I did once so prize this flocking and herding together in shallow liveliness that I did sell my soul to get it."

Presently songs broke out here and there. A zither tinkled, and a quartette of men's voices swung into a strongly rhythmic mountain melody. Across Vroni's face danced a sudden light of youth and carelessness. She smiled at her brother in gay reminiscence of the home country. Her childhood gleamed in her luminous eyes, and for the moment the sad years were as naught.

The zither was swept to the ground with a crash, followed by shouts of angry expostula-

tion. A man strode forward, shook his fist
in menace, pointed, uttered imprecations and
ribald words.

At the first sound of his voice, Vroni's face
became rigid, while inwardly she cowered and
shrank as under physical blows.

Truths, Vincenz Berg was telling, hideous
truths — gesticulating wildly, advancing un-
steadily, stopped by the tables. It was to
Vroni as if she were exposed nude, body
and soul, before that throng, — whether moments or hours she knew not.

As in a dream, she saw another figure standing in the little space in the centre of the
room, a tall fellow with a tow head; and,
through her fright and the hammering in
her temples rattled in idiotic repetition a
meaningless haunting thing of long ago:

" The enemy is approaching, the enemy, the
enemy — over the bridge, the enemy — approaching — the enemy — enemy — enemy."

Calm and distinct above all noise and mur-
murings, she heard Tiber call to mine host : —

"Cousin Wilhelm, this man is drunk and
raving sheer craziness. Let us put him
out."

But before Cousin Wilhelm could emerge

from his barricade of beer-barrels, and take active part in the procedure, the man was distinctly and very neatly out — and not immediately did Tiber reappear. Nodding good-humoredly to those who spoke to him as he was regaining his place, he remarked carelessly, and without a glance toward Vroni's corner : —

"'Tis naught. *Schnapps* makes rare crazy jabber. Let us sing."

Melchior, whose blood had curdled with horror, was recovering himself sufficiently to reckon chances. The zither was tinkling cheerily again. The august group in which he sat seemed unconscious that a vulgar disturbance had the temerity to compromise any person in their immediate society. One whose back was turned to the room remarked superbly : —

"One of them Social Democrats, most likely, strayed in here by mistake," and had never deigned to turn his head as Berg went flying by.

Melchior wondered feebly if all were strangers, as might be the case, or if, by ill-luck, some present happened to know his sister's story. He dared not speak to her. He wriggled on his chair. He wished she would not look so ghastly pale. It would attract attention from those who otherwise might not suspect she had been implicated. He felt most truly wretched, and almost failed to answer when an under-butler spoke. Jakobine hitched her chair inch by inch away from Vroni, who had not stirred, and seemed scarcely to breathe.

How long she sat thus, she had no idea. She looked at no one. It was all in vain. She could never again be acceptable among decent men and women. The world was blind, unfair, and deadly cruel, but too strong for her. Amid the merriment and jingling glasses, blank desolation encompassed her, and a terrible sense of the utter emptiness of life. Vincenz's unforeboded return had been so cruelly sudden her spirit was quite broken. She waited, irresolute, longing to flee, dreading to move. Her seat happily was near the entrance door. At length, while a well-tempered burst of laughter occupied the board, she stole out, and Melchior and Jakobine, wise as the serpent, appeared not to notice her exit.

She went a short distance, and leaned, trembling, against a building. Hearing a step behind her, she shuddered; but it was a straight firm step, and she breathed again.

"Thou, Vroni!" exclaimed a joyful voice, and Tiber grasped both her hands. For many moments she stood still with closed eyes.

"So! 'T is enough," she muttered curtly, stood erect and straightened her bonnet. "I have not thanked thee, Tiber. Seest, I cannot. Wast ever a good heart, and so, good-night to thee."

With a fair show of resolution she started on her way.

"Nay, Vroni, not so shallst thou shake me off after long years," he began, stumbling a little at the start — his old trick — though in the room just now he had spoken with placid ease. "Now thou art come again" — a great glad ring in his voice — "I be minded, God willing, never more to let thee go. By thy leave I shall walk home with thee. 'T is wiser for sundry reasons. And that I may not do as once I did, fearing my own poor words, and ever rare shamefaced before thee, I ask straightway, willst be my wife?"

Like a man laying aside a heavy load, he exhaled a huge breath of relief.

"There, 't is out, *Gottlob!* I pray thee,
Vroni, answer not too speedily. Of thy
speedy answer I do fear me ere I have said my
say. Seest, art a far too tidy maid for me.
Am but a dullish fellow for one like thee.
Doubt not that I do know it. Nay, speak not
yet, Vroni, for if I be stopped in my rare run
of speech mayhap I ne'er can get in pace
again. 'T is nigh on six years since I did see
thy face, but have been serving for thee ever
since — like Jacob in the Holy Bible for his
tidy maid the Rachel. For I 've done all that
thou didst say that night. Did leave Count
Benno's service on the grounds thou didst
point out. Did turn them over in my mind
and find them wise. For joiner-work am not
unhandy, and first did lean that way, and
searched but found no chance. So most
soberly did sit me down and think it out that
the best of me being my good legs, they best
would serve me as profession. But were it
not for thee, I 'd not be postman and promoted
twice, and for that I have to thank thee and
none else. Of much I have to tell thee,
Vroni, but 't will keep. Seest, am mortal
slow, but steady and getting on, and fond of
thee, — ah, Vroni, canst believe! since the

day I first did see thee, full seven years gone,
at Waldmohr. *So ist's.* Willst have me,
Vroni?"

"Hast quite lost thy sense? Didst not hear
that man?"

"Mind not what that fool spake! None did
mind or list or know or care. Fear naught."

" 'T was true, Tiber, every word."

" I know it — damn him!" returned the big
fellow, a sob in the throat. Doubling a stout
fist, he extended his right arm once or twice
straight before him in the night. "Willst be
my wife, Vroni?"

" Nay, Tiber, never."

"Dost like somebody?" he asked in alarm.

" I care but for one man, and he is dead —
my father."

"Would I had known him," said Tiber,
gently. " I mind me every word thou once in
joy didst speak of him. In thy grief I did
think of thee many a time, Vroni — but saw
thee not, Count Benno sending me no more
to town. 'T was sorrow and vexation; but
now art come again!" he cried with irrepres-
sible rejoicing. " Have missed thee so sore.
Was spying ever for thee in the streets, in
every crowd, and for thy name on letters. To

two towns — 't was long ago — I hied me finding out your whereabouts, but — take it not ill
— vex not thyself — "

"Nay, Tiber," she said wearily, "speak out,
I pray thee."

"Each time I did spy *him* there before me,
and heavy of heart did turn about and go."

She groaned.

"Then, since I might not see thy face, I did
thy work that thou didst give me. Seest,
Vroni, in the Post 't is not all legs. 'T is
somewhat head. Must learn there too, and
read, and write reports, and cipher. They
put one in new branches. Mayhap 't is on
the train, mayhap off in a village, or with
the parcels, or at stamping all the night. A
man must learn all sides of it, that each may
lend a hand when there be pressure. I'll
tell thee what I'd tell no other. Ofttimes
when I must drive a new thing into my thick
pate, it seems just to take marrow out of me.
Did I not hang on, and give me deadly pains,
I'd get naught at all of that which other men
do catch in play and lightness."

"Tiber, thou art no mean man. Truly I do
respect thee," she broke out quickly, with a
touch of her old manner.

" Thy respect is good coin, Vroni; yet, by
Saint Peter and Saint Paul, respect's not all I
make so bold as to crave from thee. Wast
my little schoolmaster. Didst set me tasks
and tell me truths, but put in me stoutheart-
edness. Without thee I had been a block, a
lump. Without thee I had never worked
upon thy matters each hour I did get. Until
then, in Count Benno's service I did hang
about much time and yawn. So without thee
I had not later what was needed in my tow
head — didst call me Towhead — dost mind
thee of it? — for the work that suits me well.
For the racing and the running in all weathers,
I do like, and am greeted of many folk in
kindly wise, and the children on my rounds
make friends with me and spring with shouts
to meet me. Hast done a good work on me.
But 't is for something else I want thee. Wast
a brave little schoolmaster, yet not for that art
thou so dear. Wast ever in my heart — so
deep, so firm, so warm. Say, Vroni, willst
be my wife?"

" Truly art thou duller than I did think,"
she answered with sad effort, " yet dull in
naught save one thing only. Mayhap silence
were wiser. If I do answer thee at all, 't is

but to convince thee of thy great lack of reason."

" 'T is well, Vroni. Convince."

She enumerated the world's arguments, one by one, against herself. No enemy could have been more severe.

" 'T is naught. It hath no meaning."

She painted in careful colors the girl he ought to marry.

"I like her not," he rejoined calmly. "I like but thee. Nor saw I ever anywhere one fit to wipe dust off thy shoes. Am dull, mayhap, in all things else save that I do see thee as thou art, and have the grace to love thee with all strength and warmth. Willst marry me?"

She sought to show him, rather brokenly, for she felt weary and heartsick, how futile was his hope; spoke of the children and the consecration of her life to them; hinted at the sentiments with which a man would be apt to regard such children, so beloved by her.

He laughed a mellow laugh of incredulity.

"Thou, Vroni, 't is not thine own wise way of talk. Me, hating children!"

"And never aught of peace of mind, since scenes like that which did to-night affright me might blast me any hour."

" That 's *my* business," he muttered grimly. " Be thou at rest."

" 'T is my bad head coming on, Tiber, or truly my words would better and more strongly warn thee, as they in duty should, and thou wouldst plainly see thy great unwisdom, which any fool could tell thee."

" He were in truth a fool that did attempt it ! "

" Tiber, dost mind thee of the enemy — the enemy ? "

" If I do mind me ! "

" They gallop over all bridges in my brain this night so that my thought is lame and weary."

" Dear head ! Would I might rest it where I would ! And would thou gavst me leave this night to take on the morrow to the Rathhaus one of my fifty sheets, — clean penned and without flies, — on which is plainly writ our two names joined as those who do mean wedlock."

" Tiber," she said in deep emotion and astonishment, " familiar though thou be, 't is a new man that I do see in thee. I know thee, yet I know thee not."

" Truly 't is no less in my own mind the case," he returned with a little laugh, " for I

do ever marvel at myself and at my trickling
speech, and am as one newborn. 'T is the
gladness. So I do ask thee still once more,
willst be my wife?"

"Thou knowst it cannot be. Bid me good-
night and leave me now. This is the house.
I thank thee from my heart for thy good service and thy trustiness. I bid thee good-bye
and God-speed, for in kindness am I minded
to see thee no more."

"*Na, na!* 'T is a bit speedy, Vroni! 'T will
never do. Must see, thyself, thou shouldst
not fret a good friend so. For that I be —
thy good friend; though more beside — by
the Kaiser's beard I deny it not!"

As she said nothing, he went on presently
with a certain insidious boyishness: —

"Thou, Vroni, I did make some little things
for thee, boxes and shelves in wood with carving, and everywhere a curly *I*. 'T is the
prettiest letter of them all, and works in rarely
well. The toys are nigh enough to furnish a
house, for many a night these many years did
I sadly turn to them for comfort. 'T is naught,
mayhap; yet I'll not lie — 't is tidy work
enough. Say, Vroni, when may I come, only
to show thee such a little box?"

Low and strained, she answered:

"Seest, Tiber, I can bear no more."

He took her hands in his firm grasp:

"'T is true that in my gladness I do seem to have small thought of grievous things that weigh on thee. And I would have thee glad likewise, not mindful of old pain. Yet think not I lack the heart to understand thy thought. Though ciphering figures be not yet my way to take mine ease, oh, trust me, Vroni, for thee have I quite other wits. And must I touch upon that I fain would bury out of sight," — he paused an instant, his tone lower, very firm, the light from the great lamp over the gate falling full on his manly face, — "'t is only this I'll say: had I a lamb, or such like little thing and did some sudden evil beast, a wolf or such, wound it and hurt it sore, would I then anger me with the lamb? So, that there be no mistake, I ask thee, Vroni, willst be my wife?"

She looked at him intently for some moments, and answered with poignant sadness:

"Mayhap 't was no lamb; mayhap 't was no wolf—yet art a brave man, Tiber," and slipped through the gateway.

XVIII

"WAS it a blow I fairly did deserve must bear it stoutly and whimper not.   Did I deserve it not then surely can I bear it. Whether desert or not desert and how long the heart must writhe for old misdeeds — 't is the *Herr Gott's* business."

For weeks after Vincenz's attack, thus reasoned Vroni, day in, day out.   Her argument seemed sound; nevertheless, after the manner of greater philosophers, she suffered from heart throes and depression.   Of Vincenz she saw no more, but dreaded him perpetually, and relapsed into her old condition of nervous apprehension.   Withal, she was discontented with herself, craving affection, thinking oftener of Tiber than was consistent with her theories, and, worst grief of all, perceiving no way to secure her children.   Now that Vincenz was lowering, she determined more than ever to have them with her, vaguely fearing him.   Who could foresee what he

in some fit of irresponsible rage, as recently,
might undertake? They would be safe only
with her. Yet she could not transport them
from freedom to a cage in town and be absent
from them all day at her work. What then?
What, indeed?

On a chance half-holiday she walked
through busy streets, and pondered ways and
means, all ineffectual. As she passed, rigidly
plain in dress, and absorbed in thought, people turned to look at her, and turned again.
Most of them had no idea why their wandering gaze grew suddenly intent; but now and
then a painter gave her an explicitly searching glance, and, were he so inclined, could
have informed them that in her clear-eyed,
straight-featured face lay a rare calm and
a reserve of power which amid the shifting
throng arrested and surprised attention.

Moving on aimlessly, she stopped an instant
before a broad window where a gleam of color
attracted her half-unconscious sense; and her
somewhat mechanical gaze merged into a soft,
half sad smile of recognition. She remained
some minutes rooted there. In her deep
hypnosis was nothing at which the passers-by
could wonder, for she stood where a perennial

group of Lot's wives was wont to block the pavement, and plunge into that rapt contemplation created in some minds exclusively by bonnets.

Vroni beheld but one object, — a picture, a memory, a vision; in point of fact, merely a bunch of silk and velvet sweet peas, in many shades of violet, lying upon a piece of old gold plush. Her expression became singularly alert. She glanced up at the sign, which with chaste simplicity announced *Laure*. A series of keen observations embraced various details. When she turned from that window, she had again taken her fate into her own hands, and beneath the resolution visible upon her countenance, lurked a small spark of rather diabolical humor.

Not many weeks later, the somnolent Melchior, steering the yawning royal gondola through a crowded thoroughfare, happened to see, on a prominent square crossed by many streets, a new shop, or rather an old shop with new appointments, for it was taking on whiteness with rare and discreet touches of gold. On a breezy corner flanked by rows of excellent and sedate business houses, it began to assume a peculiar daintiness, and an almost exotic charm. Each day he drove up, observing it from afar, and deigned to regard its developments with ever-increasing interest. Large plate-glass windows replaced more ordinary ones, and manifold changes seemed to be going on in the structure of the interior. Melchior was conscious of a rather ignoble curiosity, for a man in his position, as to the nature of the business demanding this mild resplendence of environment. Pictures, he presumed.

Presently a sign went up, VÉRONIQUE, in gold and white. At this foreign name good Melchior stared with benevolent unconsciousness. Thereafter, the chief windows displayed a mass of old gold plush, artistically rumpled round a centre-piece of snowy linen, upon which appeared each day, with a few fresh flowers, a new scheme of decorative and tempting viands — a charming still-life effect. When Melchior beheld a fine fat capon carved and re-adjusted, an ancient bottle in its honorable raiment of dust and cobwebs, a glass half filled with mellow Pommard, and a bunch of purple grapes lying negligently near: —

"*Potztausend!*" he remarked. "Who'd

have suspected a cook! But 't is in grand
style and noble to make your mouth water."

More and more, driving leisurely toward
the shop, from one or another of various long
approaches, he enjoyed the sight of its white
and distinguished prominence. As on one
occasion he was turning slowly past it into a
side street, he shot through the open doors
one of his swift oblique glances of explora-
tion and had he not been sustained by the
habit of strict propriety would have tumbled
down in a heap from his box. For he looked
straight into the quizzical eyes of his sister
Vroni, who nodded carelessly to him, as though
she had been bowered all her life in white
and gold, turned her back and went on, appar-
ently giving instructions to a group of maids
capped and aproned like herself.

Despite his emotional uproar, he continued
to haunt that dreaded spot which exerted an
irresistible fascination upon him. From a
side door, he saw two brown and handsome
children emerge with a young nursery maid,
and start off for a walk. He followed them,
noted their hours, in suburban streets often
walked his grand equipage close to the pavement, heard their prattle, and his heart felt

as dull and empty as the majestic ark in his
wake.

Vroni's first patron the young assistants
thought an odd sort of customer. It was a
beautiful and great lady, whose hands Madame
Véronique kissed repeatedly and as quick as
a flash. Then madame led the lovely lady
into the little private room which looked
upon the garden where the children played.
When after a long time the two came out, the
lady's eyelids were pink under her veil, and
madame accompanied her straight out to the
carriage. That day the lady ordered nothing,
but came soon again, and took Nita and Dion
out in the woods with her; often she called
for them; often she stayed long in the private
room; and many orders came from her, and
from her fine friends.

Melchior reported the Frege horses standing frequently and long at Vroni's door.

"Ha!" exclaimed his Jakobine, with wifely
explicitness, "the jackanapes comes bouncing
up like a very *Hans Wurst!* Yet," eying her
spouse malevolently, "there be mettle in her
which I do not mislike. Would all her kin
had her backbone."

Vroni's second customer was of another

type. When madame, coming in, saw him sitting at a little table in the corner, the young maids noted that she colored rosy-red, and sent them promptly to their tasks.

Tiber, gravely but with a twinkle in his eye, continued to take minute sips of coffee, and to watch her benignly over his tiny cup.

"Shouldst not come here," she began, with coolness and decision. "Knowst I did plainly tell thee my meaning."

Somewhat wistful, perturbed by her manner, he stared at her a moment; but, taking counsel within himself, he returned after rather long deliberation:—

"Vroni, didst respectfully invite the public to try thy fine cookery. If a postman be not the public, I pray thee, then, who is?"

The entrance of customers postponed her reply. Regularly at a certain hour every day, appeared white Tiber, good-humored and serene, sipped his nectar with incredible slowness, and surveyed her to his heart's content. On days when he could afford the time, he prolonged his bliss by devouring an incredible number of cakes. There was no chance for private conversation in her well-filled rooms, but across tables and strangers' heads

much was mutely discussed between the two.
She sometimes heard both children, even
Dion, who was apt to be ungracious to
strangers, shout "Uncle Tiber!" before the
door. The maid in charge related that he
often walked with them a short bit. Of all
this Vroni thought her share, yet had little
time to dwell succinctly upon the future, so
exhaustively did her bold venture absorb her
powers.

It was, indeed, a great venture, for at the
start she had to risk her little capital. But
she prospered beyond her most sanguine ex-
pectation. Her fine cookery shop reached
rich harvests. She worked early and late,
served dainties, lunches, and French dinners
within and without the house. Her energy,
elasticity, inspiration, and genius for organi-
zation seemed inexhaustible, now that Nita
and her Dion were within reach of her arms.
Her suite of pleasant rooms speedily became
a place of fashionable resort for afternoon
tea, and her kitchen, in vista, was a sort of
grill room bright with blue and white tiles,
and gleaming metal, while she and her corps
of pretty and clever-looking maids commanded
the situation with calm ease.

Count Benno and his clanking comrades honored her with orders, often with their presence, and vowed she was *"pyramidal."* She provided grand dinners for the embassies. Praises not only of her cuisine, but of her judgment, shrewdness, immense experience, and taste, as well as of her straight dealings, sounded on all sides. People greatly approved her manners, too, and the discreet tone of her establishment. One knew at once, they said, with what kind of woman one was dealing, which was such a comfort in these degenerate days. Her serious investigation of the character and quality of guests at projected dinners, her respectful attitude toward her business, and many of her remarks were cited as original and amusing. She was considered a rather unique personality.

The height of youthful feminine ambition was to be married at St. Ambrosius and have Véronique do the breakfast. A high personage at Court remarked it was a mystery to him, how the town had existed so long without her, for when she arrived, it was obvious she had simply to slip into the place which had always been waiting for her genius. Melchior, at this epoch, drew up his horses to ask

the children if they were aware he was their
uncle. Nita affably accepted him forthwith,
but Dion, with a stare of haughty disapproval,
declared he "believed it not."

Across this prosperity lay a black shadow.
Sometimes it stealthily followed the children.
It had walked, too, behind her, when for some
special festival she had gone to inspect a
dining-room, for, as the Japanese their flowers,
she arranged dinners with exquisite adjust-
ment to the essential meaning of their environment. The shadow cultivated the habit
of standing at her windows and peering in,
with a distasteful and faded jauntiness. It
seemed a shadow of sinister omen, and it
appalled her. There were nights when she
lay sleepless, mourning bitterly that she never
could escape from the past.

In her private room where were her desk,
ledger, and various account-books, was a
nearly life-sized photograph of the weaver at
his loom. She possessed, among her few
relics of him, a rude tin-type made by a
pedler, in return for his dinner. He had proposed to take her, but she gleefully piloted
him into the front room, and captured her
father. The artist to whom she gave her

order had wrought the reproduction and enlargement with peculiar sympathy and skill. Dionysius, in soft lines and plastic modelling, occupied nearly one whole wall. The genius of the place, he confronted, with deep eyes and kindly but direct questioning, every one who crossed the threshold.

Sitting in her low chair, her head thrown back upon her hands, Vroni, late at night, as was her wont, wistfully communed with the weaver.

"What willst from me? Dost ask something with thine eyes. Yet smilst as though thou fain would say, 'My foolish Mädel.' Truly, 't is so. In which thing then be I most foolish? 'T is Vincenz surely, that thou meanst, for he doth try me and affright me sorely, fearing I know not what. 'T is a grievous and mean condition to be sore afraid. Would I knew how to end it! I take it there be a remedy for all ills, did one know how to find it."

Tranquil, half amused, the weaver looked up from his work and contemplated her. Ever searching for his message, she gazed thoughtfully into the life-like picture-eyes.

"Smilst. 'T is little worth, 't is naught; —

is that thy meaning?" With a great start of
self-conviction: "Dost mean I did ever make
great talk of scorn for cowards, yet do shiver
and shake myself? Meanst there 's naught in
life worth such affright? And Vincenz is
but a mortal man, no more, no less? *Ach,
Väterle,* hast right and reason. I 'll do it —
what thou meanst. 'T is a bitter pill, but
worse ones did I swallow many and ofttimes.
At any rate, 't is ill to hoot at others, yet for
months and years to fear and quake. Truly
do I shame myself, and wonder much."

In spite of her brave convictions, she sighed
from time to time, and was sick at heart as
she considered her course of action.

One rainy day, the first time she again saw
Vincenz haunting the precincts, she went to
the door, bade him good-morning, and asked
him to come in. With a look as if he doubted
whether he had heard aright, he followed her
to her room, where the weaver's eyes met him
as he entered, and impressed him unpleasantly.

Vroni, very pale, remarked: —

"I have to speak with thee. But first, perhaps, thou 'llt taste this to refresh thee. 'T is
the coffee Véronique of which, doubtless,
thou hast heard."

Pushing the cup aside, he said, with a faint sneer:—

"Art in a snug nest."

"Truly," she answered in a calm voice, but her hands trembled.

"Canst laugh at a poor fool whose life thou didst ruin, unless it be that in thy good luck thou mostly dost forget."

"I laugh not, Vincenz, and forget not."

"What willst say or do, that thou didst stoop to call me in? Am little minded to believe it be for love," he added bitterly, "though knowing thee, one knows not what strange whim may mount into thy head."

She moved abruptly, and said somewhat curtly:—

"Art right, Vincenz. 'T is not for love."

"For all that I do know," he flung in suspicious jealous fashion at her, "'t is to mock me. Yet canst not mock in all things. 'T is my will to see my children. I am their father. Show me them."

Vroni rose and with a rigid hand grasped a chair-back. Anticipating a refusal he assumed a hostile and threatening air. But she, to his amazement, replied in a low and strongly controlled voice:—

"Art their father and shalt see them. 'T is one reason why I bade thee to come in."

She turned to call them, stopped, looked back imploringly at him, deadly anxiety, prayer, and warning seeking utterance; but restraining them all, she said only, — turning again, her hand upon the door: —

"I do pray thee, Vincenz, to be minded they be very young and till this moment, happy."

For reply he drummed with his fingers on the table, and smiling with a touch of the old complacency looked out the window.

Nita advanced graciously, gave him her hand, and asked with the air of one embarrassed by riches in this respect: —

"Which of my nuncles is it?"

Vroni hesitated.

"A friend," she said.

"Hast forgot thy coffee, Nuncle Friend," Nita reminded him. "Hast not plenty sugar?"

Vincenz smiled slightly upon the charming little person but cared no more for her because the boy, standing apart and scowling, roused the man's spirit of conquest.

"Willst not come to me?"

Beneath a mass of overhanging curls, Dion's great sombre eyes peered out like a wild thing's under a bush.

"Nay, I like thee not," he answered, and to all solicitation remained obdurate.

Vroni stood waiting, passive, mistrust and fear strong within her. She loathed the thought that Vincenz could lay his hand on Dion. Her instinct was to snatch him up and flee with him. Suddenly she became aware of her wild notions, and that Vincenz at the moment wore no formidable but a weary and singularly disconcerted air.

"If thou do play to him," she said softly, "wilt win him fast enough. 'T is in the nursery — his piano."

Dion stood motionless by the player, gradually drew nearer, laid his head against Vincenz's shoulder and when he rose slipped a confiding hand in his, and led him back to Vroni's room.

"Go now to Brigitte, little ones."

"Good-bye, Nuncle Friend," piped Nita.

"Mayst play to me again on my piano," said Dion, solemnly.

"Had I them and thee I were a better man," began Vincenz, moodily, and meeting the singular eyes of the man on the wall, glanced uneasily out the window.

"Mayhap, but I do doubt it. 'T is thy meaning at the moment, but at the doors of every gin-shop, loiter little children waiting to lead their fathers home. Hast other children who did ne'er prevail on thee in any wise. Nay, Vincenz, be not fierce with me. 'T is far from my intent to vex thee. I fain would but answer thee with sense and truth. Nor can aught uproot the thought in me, which doth grow firmer every day I live, that 't is only one's own heart, plodding sternly, that doth by slow degrees gain strength against itself — with Heaven's help," she added to herself, "in ways that be most marvellous."

"Hast it so good about thee, canst well afford thy wisdom," he retorted in dull rage; for she was still desirable because beyond his reach, the remote compassion of her voice irritated him, and the comfort of her surroundings mocked his inability to share it. "Dost live in plenty. Hast even thine own serving maids to wait on thee; while I, 't is true, am fallen, and no more that which I was of old."

"I have no servants, seeing I do work the

most and largest. I do but train, from my
experience, my blithe apprentices for their
life-work. Vincenz, I do spy thy thought
which, trust me, is unsound. Were I with
thee I'd ne'er have had these rooms which
much do busy thy reflection. When thou
dost turn that in thy mind, willst see the
straightness of its reasoning. Nor is it sense
for me to dwell on that which I and the children might have been with thee, since 't is
but sheer imagining. 'T is other business I
would bespeak with thee."

"In truth, I were right curious to hear it,"
he muttered sullenly, regarding her despondently, yet with vague expectancy.

She moistened her lips and throat with a
swallow of the untouched cold coffee, and
looked one instant at the weaver.

"Vincenz, for some things I have to thank
thee, for others I do crave thy pardon."

With a bound he straightened himself and
stared with widely opened eyes.

"I did fear thee. 'T was a wrong to thee
and me. I fear thee no more. I did hate
thee. I hate thee no more. For fearing and
hating thee I do shame myself, and pray thee
pardon me. New thoughts of thee are come

— are sent to me. I see thee otherwise. Art
but a mortal man, Vincenz, and I am minded
't is a blame to fear aught on earth — save sin.
Art not too happy. Would I could see thee
brave and cheery at thy work again. Didst
have a liking for me once — "

She hesitated. Vincenz had shaded his
eyes with his hands. In her face was a poignant mournfulness.

"Well, as to that," she went on, low and
sadly, "I fain would thank thee for all of
good in thy affection. I do thank thee for
gentle hours many a time. For the rest, I
do hold thee not wholly without mercy to be
blamed. 'T is a hard matter to disentangle
threads of right and wrong that ofttimes do
mix themselves most wondrously, and what be
wrongest in this world — *na*, men roar loud
where the *Herr Gott* keeps silence. But this
I 'll say, Vincenz, I take it there be somewhat
to plead for thee, both by way of thy quick-
silver nature and the poor breeding they did
hang on thee. And whatever blame be mine
by right — how much, how little, I discuss
not, neither do I measure — I do now take
upon myself. I hate thee not. I wish thee
well. *So ist's.*"

The man had buried his head in his arms upon the table and was sobbing heavily, nor was she quite dry-eyed.

After some time, he raised his head, and said gently: —

"'T is probable that thou dost mean to marry."

"Leastwise, I do weigh that matter."

"Then canst no longer wish me well."

Touched by his submission, she replied: —

"Nay, henceforth I wish thee well. And if I do marry, which may or may not be, 't is a just man — juster than any I have known, save one."

After a long pause, he asked humbly: —

"Is it thy meaning I may ever come to greet thee, if I be mindful to vex thee no more? Forget thee, Vroni, can I never, and — I did like the cloudy little kid."

"Take it not ill that I do say thee nay," she returned with great gentleness. "Seest, Vincenz, it were painful, and rarely awkward at this present; nor can I wholly trust thy flickering mood, which now is light, and in a moment, darkness. But this I tell thee straight and sure. Art thou ill or in need I 'll be thy friend. Dost turn from drink and

slippery ways, I 'll rejoice—none more. Dost
look about and try to comfort where thou
hast caused much misery, — dost have some
care of children joyless through thee, yet on
whom thou in sheer carelessness didst bestow
the gift of life, I 'll honor thy endeavor. Yet
dost thou naught of this, art thou wrong and
wretched, I 'll not turn wholly from thee.
I 'll be fair to thee, and seek no more to forget thou art the father of my children. In
time, 't is my most firm intent to tell them
all. I am minded neither to speak nor act
lies to them, God helping me. In time, mayhap, I will receive thee. I promise naught.
I but say mayhap. On thine own self doth
that depend. Yet once more say I strongly,
I do wish thee well. Canst, if thou willst,
set thy teeth hard and be a man. Go now,
Vincenz. Trust somewhat to the years that
ofttimes do work in mercy for us. God speed
thee. *Lebewohl.*"

XIX

TIBER'S queer blondness, shabby blue uniform, and placid, somewhat humorous observation entrenched themselves no longer behind Liliputian mocha-cups and ramparts of tiny cakes. His corner was vacant many days; none had seen him; Vroni missed him acutely, and when late one evening he was announced, and shown into her sanctum where she sat writing, not penning, to Armand Gireaud, her heart began to beat rather fast.

Tiber, unsmiling, sad indeed, seemed to enter with a definite purpose. He sat down and seemed about to divulge it, when he was arrested by the consciousness of the presence of a third party. Long and in silence he looked at the weaver.

"Art strangely like him," he said very gravely, and sighed.

"What hast thou, Tiber? Art little like thyself."

"Vroni, have come to take my leave of thee."

" Art going away? " she said slowly.

"Nay, but," after a pause, "I do give thee up."

She sat quite still and eyed him steadily.

" 'T is wise," she returned at length. " 'T is doubtless very wise. 'T is as I bade thee," but her tone was lifeless.

" Surely art not surprised ? "

" It matters little if I be surprised or no, since I do tell thee thou dost act most wisely." Her voice was toneless and her approval numb.

He leaned forward, in his good face great trouble and yearning : —

" Why shouldst thou be surprised? Art so clear in thy mind. Dost surely right well see my case. I had not thought to speak it out, it stands writ so plain before all eyes that thou art now a dame too great and fine and rich for me."

" *Sapristi !* " she ejaculated softly.

Poor Tiber could not look at her and say what he had to say, so he contemplated the weaver, whose kindliness encouraged him.

" When I did find thee I did thank my God. Nor was I too dismayed by the cool welcome, so sorely much had hurt thee first and last.

The hope within me was strong enough for
ten men in like case. Was so bold as already
to cast mine eye on cottages, and did spy one
building on the outskirts, nigh to fields and
meadows for the children. For I do earn, if
humbly, yet enough to keep a wife and thrifty
house. Thou didst see me march in here in
brave humor, not abashed. And at the first,
did slyly praise myself for my methods, and
saw things straight before me, and had great
joy and pride in thee and thy good management. But as I came and came, and saw thee
great thyself among the great, the truth began
to dawn on me."

"What great marvel hast discovered?" she
murmured, her elbows on the table, her chin
on her clasped hands, her face soft, inviting,
tenderly quizzical.

But he, his grave eyes always uplifted, went
steadily on with his tale : —

"Moreover the little maid Brigitte, in great
pride of thee, did make known to me what
thou hast done for thy sister on the Alp."

"Ha, we needs must muzzle that mouth-
piece !"

"Brigitte did relate with glee how that her
mother and her lame tailor father and the many

many children were living in the cottage by
what she did call the Witch Tooth, and had
naught to pay save to keep things straight.
That thou through a man of law hast bought
the place for a goodly sum of thy brother
Sebastian, thy brother Melchior approving,
and neither did know the purchaser. That
then through thy man of law hast let repairs
be made and all claims paid, and a spacious
wing be added for room and comfort's sake."

" Ha, 't is not a kingly pleasure-Schloss ! "
and Vroni smiled through a sudden shimmer,
yet seemed half ashamed. " Seest, Tiber,"
she pleaded deprecatingly, "the deed's far
less than thy words do sound. 'T is plain
living on our Alp. Yet I do love it every
inch, and could not see the old place pass to
strangers. Fain would I have my children
wild and frolicsome there in summer-time;
and when the town grows stifling-tame, and I
do pine for space and winds, and homesickness is strong on me, fain would I turn me to
the hills."

Tiber watched her as she spoke, but looked
off, continuing : —

" Hearing the same, I did seem to get a chill
and hollowness in my inside. 'Willst wed a

capitalist,' said I to myself, 'thou that art of
the plain folk and of no account?' Then the
little maid in chirping pride did boast to me
what thou didst earn last month. That sum
did knock me flat. Straightway I hied me
home, and there did pound my head in rage,
and cry, 'Wast e'er a dolt and fool, and stay'st
it all thy life.'" Turning toward her he added
firmly, "Beside all which, 't is unseemly a
man do hang upon the earnings of his wife.
Hast heard. *So ist's.*"

Vroni had risen as he spoke, and drawn ever
nearer, smiling, smiling; stood close to him,
put two hands on his shoulders, and, many
swift shades of feeling working in her face,
said tremulously: —

"Towhead, I be minded thou and I much
do beat about the bush. Is my great wealth
thine only pain, canst be easy in thy mind.
Does naught else hold us twain apart 't were
a blame on us to make a mountain of a mole-
hill. 'T is true much gold passeth through
my hands, but I must needs spend largely to
keep my great machine in running order. For
my children shall I hoard only in modesty and
simple reckoning. So cruel be I not as to
steal from their future lives the needs of

hearty work — which is a help and blessing. For the rest, we will promptly use for others, as we do go along, the most that I may earn, — in ways of which we 'll later speak, wherein thy sense and trustiness will greatly serve the purpose. So much for the money that doth so vastly awe thee, to thy shame, say I. Did hold thee to be braver. Hast made me say outright: ' Towhead, will take thee, if so be thou 'llt take me.' "

The latter half of her speech was more or less muffled and interrupted. Much and long they spoke that night, but longer were their long silences.

" So take it not ill that I do look at marriage with mine own eyes," said Vroni, at the close of some recital, " and 't is fair to say to thee, Tiber, that much as I do trust thee and our chance of peace together, prove we not true companions, I for thee and thou for me, I should hold it baseness to house together."

He regarded her with benevolent irony:

" Ha, Vroni, willst divorce me ere the knot be tied? "

" 'T is but my thought I fain would tell thee."

" So God will, we shall have time for telling thoughts."

"Seest, Tiber, I do love thee well, and trust thee utterly, yet would not rush blindly —"

"*Na!* Hast the face to call this rushing!" he protested with a queer grimace. "'T will be a decade soon since I first did court thee."

She smiled but persisted: —

"Have worked my way and thought my thoughts alone, and pray thy patience do I plainly say thou shalt be my friend and comrade, my loving husband and my dear. But not even thou canst with the gift of thy good name change aught of good or ill in my past life. And 't is for no protection that I do marry thee. Hast heard?"

He took her face between his hands and scrutinized it fondly: —

"Ah, Vroni, Vroni, canst not yet believe I understand thee?" he murmured with great tenderness, adding, after a moment: "Yet since the Lord did make me big and burly, willst not vex thy dear heart overmuch, be I so bold as to hold an umbrella over thee 'gainst stormy weather?"

"Truly, that much I'll take not ill. Art the sort of man I like, Towhead," she murmured with emotion. "Art a brave lad."

" Ay, and good to dogs," he responded dryly.

" That we can sit and laugh !" she exclaimed.

" 'T is high time."

" I could fear having a so peaceful heart and restfulness that's new to me."

" 'T is well known the Lord takes care the trees grow not as high as the sky. Yet I fear naught, now that 't is plain I be not the fifth wheel of thy coach."

" *Ei !* Coaches and such grand connections we 'll leave to Melchior. 'T is enough for the whole kinship."

" Many a time doth he sail gloriously past my *Madame-chen's* door, I mark me. Cometh also even on his legs, my little friend Brigitte did let fall. I had not thought thy brother was possessed of legs."

" 'T was Nita took him by the hand and led him in. Poor Melchior! Ofttimes was I angered hotly with him, yet my affection clings. He hath a rare joy in the children, and for my life I know none other in his dull days. 'T were pity not to let him freshen himself with them. I did give him tea and civil greeting as to one who cometh daily — no more, no less. Likewise to his Jakobine, who soon after did march in staidly with another old tea-aunty, gave I fair courtesy, and did serve the tray myself, which I did mark was pleasing to their worships."

"Art a brave lad, Vroni, and good to dogs!"

"I fain would tell thee, Tiber, if thou wilt grant me time to speak a little sense, that Nita collects 'Nuncles,' where other children seek for butterflies and postage stamps. 'T is a motley lot."

"I know — being one of them."

"And Nuncle Crossing-Sweeper and Nuncle Bootblack, the latest whom she doth lead in sweetly for broken cakes and scraps. Nuncle Crossing-Sweeper is a friendly old man. But Nuncle Bootblack, though his dancing eyes do please me, is sorely tempted of my goodies, and it were ill-advised to leave him unmolested in my storeroom."

"Vroni."

"White Tiber?"

"Knowst all thou dost earn will belong to me?"

"What meanst?" She raised her head.

"By law,"

"Ah, yes. By law, 'T is true. I had forgot. *Na*, have already said, we'll ne'er quarrel about money."

"'T is a rarely funny old goodwife — the law," he remarked thoughtfully.

"Truly, many and ofttimes."

Presently Tiber began a low mellow laugh, and laughed on in quiet enjoyment, pausing but to chuckle again.

"Look at thee and me, Vroni, at thine work and at mine; at thine head and at my own; at thy rich earnings and at my salary; nay, more, look at all thou hast bravely done with thine own single strength; and to think the fruits of this, thy merit and thy deed, are shortly mine to have and to control, both what thou hast laid by and what thou still dost earn; thy cottage on the Alp and thy goodies in the storeroom. Truly 't is so passing droll a horse might laugh. 'T is monstrous, yet 't is law."

"'T is not the only monstrous thing and not the worst," she responded very low; and the postman drew her closer, with a larger, higher, and more manly tenderness than Count Benno von Vallade had ever felt for any woman.

"At least 't is one I shall know how to manage."

" How so? "

" By some sort of special contract, I suppose.
Am unlearned in these matters, yet know I
what be sense and what I will."

" I pray thee, Tiber! Are not thy upright-
ness and thy love stronger than any contract?
It irks me to think of promise great or small
'twixt thee and me."

" Nay, Vroni," he said firmly. " A little
chat of one thing and another I needs must
have with thy man of law. In this case I do
hold it for the best. Besides," he added, seeing
her look grave, " there be that which I fain
would have signed and sealed in my behalf.
I would buy thy cakes at thy lowest wholesale
price. Nay, more, it would appear but just
that thou shouldst grant me a commission, seeing that I did gorge myself with them in a
way that was pure advertisement for thy fine
cookery."

" My Towhead," she whispered, " my true
mate and my dear."

When, shortly, her dusty postman went
tramping out and in, great peacefulness within
his heart and upon his pleasant countenance,
lords and ladies had to wait until he met due
honors. The world thought it an odd choice

for a handsome woman like Véronique, who
with her neat income might really have looked
higher. With that business, she could have
secured a very respectable sort of merchant, or
a well-to-do if small hotel keeper. Still as Tiber
seemed to interfere not at all in her delectable
mission, the world concerned itself little with
him, and few suspected the restfulness, the
strength and beauty of their companionship.

Working girls flocked to Vroni as needles to
the magnet. She seemed always to have time
for them, and her keen insight read their na-
tures and their needs. Maids fresh from the
country and at a loss for friends and amusement, found both in her pleasant quarters;
where she tempted them with sweets, probed
their foolish hearts, steered them adroitly past
thin ice, gained their confidence and affection,
gave them good bits of happiness, and with
music and brightness tided over lonely and
dangerous Sundays. Generous to wayfarers,
kind and pitiful to sorrow and stupidity, she
had small mercy upon certain forms of careless and brutal selfishness. Occasionally her
words, with many an odd *sapristi* and *saprelotte*, fell like biting hail upon the head of
some young working man, and still more sav-

agely upon ungentle gentlemen. Often she and her towhead went late at night "fishing" in dark streets and parks. In the course of years many strange and pitiful fellow-creatures — men, women, and little children — did they find to succor and to comfort.

In their manifold quiet schemes, one other worked with them, the Comtesse Nelka. The views which they shared and which informed their endeavor would have been pronounced at Court distinctly destructive to the well-being of society. Perhaps to the extremely minute human fraction known under that head at Courts, those views may not have been inordinately flattering, but no more were they inimical; while to the vast proportion outside the pale, they were of that loving and pitiful quality that leads of necessity to unwearying brotherly deed.

The Countess von Vallade, observing now and then a mere superficial fact, thought Nelka a trifle eccentric in these matters. For what, she would like to inquire, were the numberless charitable Clubs and Societies? Besides, nothing was so unwise as to play special providence, and transplant people suddenly here and there to distant towns, and set them learn-

ing this and that. So much notice was apt to
spoil them, and such projects never turned out
agreeably and as one expected. She had no
objection to Véronique. On the contrary, she
was racy,— many found her most fascinating;
of course in her profession inimitable — unap-
proachable. That the countess had always
declared. Nor had she ever been so indis-
creet as to mention Vroni's youthful flightiness
and her *faux pas*. But Nelka seemed to go
there oftener than to her friends, too much
was too much; then some things they attempted the countess must really pronounce
excessive.

To which Nelka would respond simply: —

" Vroni and I both think we have good reason."

The countess was, in fact, not greatly exer-
cised. Nelka in her position could after all
give tone in any fashion she fancied, and a
little eccentricity was rather *chic*. Then she
neglected nothing indispensable in the way of
social functions, if she avoided much for which
the countess herself had interest.

Many painful experiences had fallen to that
lady's lot. Benno was shot in a peculiarly
ugly sort of duel, and his loss was a great grief

to them all. Knod, for certain excesses which even the army could not countenance, was cashiered. Count Vallade had resigned on account of failing eyesight. All in all, the countess could not be thankful enough that Nelka was so well established in life. Sometimes the countess said "established," sometimes "settled" or "provided for." Whatever she said, she meant that she was delighted and proud that Nelka was the wife of Baron Frege.

The countess was more than content with Nelka's society, with her gentle and affectionate consideration. There never was so devoted a daughter. Then her tact with her father. Then one of her carriages, always at the countess's disposal, — really providential, since they were obliged to give up their own. And never did the mother notice that in her presence her amiable daughter spoke of nothing near her heart.

Vroni sat smiling over a hortatory letter from Sebastian. Since wedlock had bestowed upon her a modicum of character and virtue, he was good enough to send her reams of instruction as to the management of her children. Hearing a knock, she glanced up carelessly. Comtesse Nelka, very pale and beautiful, entered, and Vroni, with one look at her face, sprang forward. Without a word, Nelka put a newspaper into her friend's hand.

Vroni gave a marked passage a swift glance, dropped upon the floor, laid her head upon the comtesse's knee, and wept passionately.

"God forgive me," she exclaimed, "but He's killed the wrong man!"

Nelka sat quite still except for a slow shiver now and then, and the soft and regular movement of her hand smoothing Vroni's hair. A stranger entering would have inferred the kneeling woman was the chief sufferer.

At length the comtesse spoke, faintly but with calm: —

"I have known it a week, Vroni. I could not come before."

Vroni sobbed on, vehement and inconsolable, muttering broken and fierce little arraignments of the deity; but, presumably, our petty notions of *lèse-majesté* do not prevail in the vast Beyond.

"Waldemar sent it with this letter," said the gentle voice. "The others do not know, — that is, I think not," she amended.

Vroni glanced at the letter, lifted the fallen paper, read the marked paragraph to the end,

and with a complete change of expression
cried : —

"A great and gallant death, — right nobly
for a friend! Ha, 't is a blame to weep for
such a man."

Nelka's smile was like nothing Vroni had
ever known except some ineffable music she
once heard.

In long retrospection the two beheld the
intricate weaving subtly woven by the years,
and were still as in a church. At last
Vroni raised her wet eyes and murmured ardently : —

"T' is braver than a hero's death, the life my
gracious, dearest comtesse lives. While Count
Vallade has his angel nigh at hand he will
never quite despair. Truly he doth wear more
of peace on his fine countenance than in the
old troublous days I do remember of, — such
rare comfort and companionship hath the poor
blind gentleman."

Nelka stooped and kissed her cheek, and
again sat motionless except for a repressed
sigh or a long shiver now and then until she
said tranquilly : —

"Dear, let me see the children one instant
before I go."

They came, Nita blithe, Dion reluctant; his thought remote, in his eyes a listening look, in his hand a crumpled bit of paper scribbled with bars and notes.

For Dion became a great musician, and out of gloom and sweetness spoke mightily to the sorrowing hearts of men.

THE END

www.ingramcontent.com/pod-product-compliance
Lightning Source LLC
Chambersburg PA
CBHW030905270326
41929CB00008B/580